1934

June 22   MacDonald, in ill health, delegates duties to Baldwin

June 28   Unemployment Assistance Boards come into being

July 19   Baldwin increases size of R.A.F.

July 31   Road Transport Act introduces driving tests and 30 m.p.h. speed limit

Sep. 9   Fascist and anti-Fascist rallies at Hyde Park

Nov. 13   Sedition Bill introduced

Nov. 20   Depressed Areas Bill introduced

1935

Jan. 28   Uproar in Commons over means test

Feb. 1   Anglo-German rearmament conference

June 7   Baldwin forms Nat. Govt.

June 18   Germans agree to a navy only one third the tonnage of Royal Navy

June 27   Peace Ballot shows strong British support for League of Nations

Nov. 14   Govt parties win 428 seats in General Election but MacDonald loses seat to Emmanual Shinwell

Dec. 9   Hoare-Laval proposals on Abyssinia denounced

Dec. 18   Hoare resigns Foreign Secretaryship

Dec. 23   Eden becomes Foreign Secretary

1936

Jan. 20   Edward VIII becomes king

Mar. 3   Military budget increases 30% to improve air defences

May 22   J. H. Thomas resigns from cabinet over budget leaks

June 23   Attlee loses censure vote on Baldwin for irresponsible foreign policy

July 21   Means test regulations revised

July 24   Jarrow special development area scheme fails

Oct. 12   Mosley leads anti-Jewish march in London's Mile End Road

Nov. 16   Edward VIII warned of damage to prestige if he marries Mrs Simpson

Nov. 31   Crystal Palace destroyed by fire

Dec. 10   Edward VIII abdicates

Dec. 11   Duke of York becomes George VI

1937

Jan. 2   Anglo-Italian agreement on Mediterranean and on independence of Spain

Jan. 14   Communists, I.L.P. & Socialist League form United Front

Apr. 24   Britain & France release Belgium from Locarno Treaty obligations

May 10–23   London bus strike

July 23   Matrimonial Causes Bill

Sep. 3   Lab. Party reiterates Britain's role in League of Nations

Sep. 10–14   Nyon Conference, called by Britain, on piracy in Mediterranean

Nov. 5   Air Raid Precautions Bill introduced in Commons

Dec. 2   Far reaching changes in British High Command

Dec. 29   New Irish constitution; Irish Free State becomes Eire

Dec. 30   Attlee visits Spain to encourage Republicans

1938

Feb. 20   Eden resigns in protest over Chamberlain's wish to agree with Italy about Spain

Feb. 21   Churchill leads attack on Chamberlain in Commons

Feb. 25   25 govt M.P.s vote against govt in unsuccessful censure motion

Apr. 16   Anglo-Italian pact on Ethiopia and Spain

Apr. 25   British 3-year agreement with Eire on outstanding disputes

July 25   Runciman reports favourably on Nazi claims in Czechoslovakia

Sep. 15   Chamberlain visits Hitler at Berchtesgaden

Sep. 27   Royal Navy mobilized

Sep. 29   Chamberlain reaches agreement on Czechoslovakia at Munich

Oct. 1   Duff Cooper resigns as First Lord of Admiralty

Dec. 1   National Register for war service started

1939

Jan. 16   Chamberlain and Halifax visit Mussolini in Rome

Feb. 27   Britain recognizes Franco's govt in Spain

Mar. 31   Britain pledges support for Poland

Apr. 27   Conscription for men of 20/21

May 23   Parliament approves plan for independent Palestine

July 9   Churchill urges military alliance with U.S.S.R.

July 11   Ministry of Supply established

Aug. 24   Parliament approves Emergency Powers Bill

[...] treaty of mutual [...]n and Daladier [...]Hitler [...]women and [...]begins [...] Bill calling up men 18–41 commits to force

Sep. 3   Britain declares war on Germany. Churchill becomes First Lord of Admiralty. *Athenia* is sunk by Germans off Ireland

Topics in Modern History Series

GENERAL EDITOR

Ivor D. Astley, B.Sc. (*Econ.*), A.C.P.
Headmaster, Hardley Secondary School, Hampshire

PEACE AND FUTURE CANNON FODDER

The Tiger: "Curious! I seem to hear a child weeping!"

Preface

Among the advantages historians enjoy are those of *selectivity* (choosing material which can highlight points in the story they wish to tell) and *labelling* periods of time with the benefit of *hindsight*.

Some ordinary and some distinguished people living in Britain between 1919 and 1939 were convinced that a second world war was inevitable but none could see like the historian in retrospect exactly when and where the division in time would be that could later allow two decades to be classified as the 'inter-war years'.

Fortunately, perhaps, the vast majority did not see themselves as living in an era chopped off by two world wars which cruelly or dramatically ended or re-shaped life for millions. Certainly, however, as the power of the dictators grew many more people became apprehensive. Newsreels of events in China and Spain and films such as H. G. Wells' 'Things to Come' frightened and affected many with the realities and foresight of terror to come from aerial bombardment.

Yet, everyday life went on. Despite the shock of the Great War, Britain was still the centre of a great Empire, and although its rôle and style were changing, Britons had many advantages.

In a succinct account, Mr Wood tells here the story of the events at home and abroad between the wars; of lost hopes of a war to end wars; of broken promises; of the new and unprecedented economic and social changes; and of dangers rapidly arising from the weaknesses of the Western democracies.

It was also a time of great cultural change. The cinema had more impact than radio, but chiefly it was a time of mass-production and—with the advent of the cheap motor car—of much greater mobility. In science and medicine too there were important discoveries and developments which were to have dramatic impact later, such as the splitting of the atom, radar, jet propulsion and man-made fibres; and pioneer work with insulin, antibiotics and penicillin.

Despite serious gaps—and especially in dealing with widespread unemployment, poverty and sickness—there was a growing social consciousness and some progress was made to alleviate commonplace suffering. For some people, they were good years; but for others—particularly at the family level—they were *insecure* years, and these were factors which figured largely among priorities to be dealt with immediately when new hope came again after the Second World War.

I. D. A.

Contents

Pg 49 Social life in 20's
Pg 4 THE STATE OF SOCIETY
Pg 19 ATTEMPT AT SOCIAL REFORM
Pg 67 Social change in the 1930's

arend

Acknowledgments

The author and publisher make grateful acknowledgment to the following for permission to reproduce illustrations detailed below:

RADIO TIMES HULTON PICTURE LIBRARY
Armistice (p.4)   *Woman voting* (p.7)   *Coal strike* (p.20)   *Coal strikers* (p.21)
Hawkers (p.22)   *After a Privy Council meeting* (p.31)   *Modern school* (p.34)
League of Nations (p.36)   *General Strike* (p.48)   *Wimbledon* (p.50)   *Factories*
(p.56)   *Unemployed* (p.58)   *Margaret Bondfield* (p.60)   *Jarrow marchers*
(p.72)   *Duke of Windsor's marriage* (p.75)   *Hitler's letter* (p.99)

POPPERFOTO
Gandhi (p.15)   *Snowden* (p.32)   *Mr & Mrs Baldwin* (p.42)   *Coal crisis
meeting* (p.47)   *Marconi & crystal set* (p.53)   *National Cabinet* (p.67)
Mussolini (p.87)   *Czech border guard* (p.97)

THE TRUSTEES & THE LONDON EVENING STANDARD
Cartoons by David Low on miners (p.49), *the Second Labour government* (p.59)
and the Spanish Civil War (p.79)

JOHN TOPHAM PICTURE LIBRARY
Advertisements (p.74)   *Road works* (p.76)

'PUNCH'
Livingstone cartoon on Ireland (p.24)   *Baumer sketch on fashion* (p.51)

FOX PHOTOS
Oswald Mosley (p.61)   *Chamberlain announces war* (p.102)

GREATER LONDON COUNCIL
Modern housing (p.33)   *Modern classroom* (p.34)

ASSOCIATED NEWSPAPERS GROUP LTD   *'Peace and Future Cannon Fodder' by
Dyson* (p.ii)

IMPERIAL WAR MUSEUM   *Body in trench* (p.1)

W.R.A.C. MUSEUM   *Q.M.A.A.C.'s dismissal* (p.5)

B.B.C.   *First cover of Radio Times* (p.45)

BRITISH LEYLAND   *Morris Minor Saloon* (p.52)

CONSERVATIVE RESEARCH DEPARTMENT   *National Government Poster* (p.64)

DAILY HERALD   *Edward's Farewell* (p.75)

THE WEINER LIBRARY   *Hitler and Hindenburg* (p.84)

REGINALD PIGGOTT   *Maps* (pp.13, 16/17, 86)

CARTOGRAPHIC ENTERPRISES   *Pictograms* (pp.109-113)

THE END OF THE GREAT WAR

During the afternoon of 11th November 1918, news began to filter through towns and villages in Great Britain that the most terrible war in the country's history had at last ended. At 11 a.m. that morning an armistice between Britain and her allies and Germany marked the final collapse of the Central Powers against whom the allies had been fighting. In towns and cities large crowds began to gather, to sing, dance and jostle one another; in the countryside smaller groups collected, often called out by the ringing of church bells. Overseas—and especially in France and Belgium—thousands of British servicemen were at last able to lay down their weapons and emerge from the trenches, shelters and dugouts in which, for four years, they had spent most of their time.

Though Britain emerged victorious from the Great War of 1914–1918, the effect on her was vast. Her French and Russian allies suffered even more, but the British had become so used to their wars being small-scale affairs involving a handful of professional soldiers and seamen that the shock of being finally caught up in a massive Continental conflict hurt very deeply. It was not just that the war lasted four years, but that it had involved Britain in pouring huge armies into Europe, spending vast quantities of money, turning industry over to war production on an enormous scale, and desperately defending her vital seaborne trade from enemy attack. Unlike the wars of the eighteenth and nineteenth century, the Great War had involved the whole country: no village was to be without its memorial to those killed in action.

The kind of war that had been fought seemed uniquely dreadful. Great battles raging for many weeks over treacherously muddy ground might result in the gain of a few hundred yards for the loss of thousands of lives. Unlike the long wars against Napoleon, the Great War showed how it had shaken up the whole of society in the way it affected leading writers and artists both during and immediately after the conflict. The experience of the Great War was to leave its mark on almost all policies followed in the inter-war period.

THE COST OF THE WAR

About three-quarters of a million British servicemen had died as a direct result of the conflict and a further million and a half had suffered seriously from wounds or gas attacks. German air and sea raids had even brought the war to British civilians to the extent of killing 1,500 of them. In 1916 the government had introduced conscription to keep up the steady flow of army recruits and this pulled in men from all over the country and from all social classes. Every community directly felt the loss of somebody's son, husband, brother or father and the whole country suffered from the loss of so many young men. It is no wonder that after 1918 the British viewed the prospect of another war with gloom and concern. The outbreak of the Great War had been greeted by cheering crowds and a rush of volunteers; the experience of the Great War destroyed any such enthusiasm for military combat.

The reality of trench warfare

The war had damaged the country's finances too. In 1914 the National Debt had stood at £650 million; by 1918 it had risen to £7,000 million as the government struggled to cope with the staggering cost of the conflict. Part of the cost of war had come from taxes. In 1914 taxation in Britain was very low indeed but by 1918 income tax had risen from ninepence in the pound to six shillings, and a whole range of taxes had been put on imports into the country. Britain had also borrowed heavily from abroad, especially from the U.S.A. to whom £850 million was owed by 1918. In fact Britain had lent more to her allies than she herself had borrowed, but 1918 found her allies quite unable to seriously repay their debts—and in the case of Russia quite unwilling even to try. Further damage to British finances came from the selling off of around ten per cent of her long-term overseas investments in order to find immediate cash for the war. This, added to the damage done by war to British shipping, insurance and banking services, meant that the country no longer obtained as much as she had done from these 'invisible' earnings.

British trade also suffered from the war. German attacks on British shipping and the need to give priority to war-supplies meant that other forms of business were neglected. Countries that had looked to Britain for supplies of manufactured goods now had to turn elsewhere, and, waiting eagerly to grab this chance were the U.S.A., Japan, and the neutral nations of Scandinavia. Losing the products of British industry encouraged foreign nations to build up their own industries instead. Even parts of the British Empire proved more interested, after 1918, in helping their own industries grow than in resuming trade with Britain.

British industry obtained some benefits from the war, and farming certainly prospered at a time when growing food at home was vital to avoid being starved as U-boats attacked food ships from abroad. The Great War was a clash between economies as well as armies, for modern warfare needed expert production of ships, guns, tanks, aircraft and explosives. Much more attention began to be paid in Britain to scientific research and to applying this to industry, whilst industries formerly neglected—like chemicals, electrical goods and glass production—now began to grow more vigorously.

Yet the war also damaged British industry. It led to more being produced by coal, iron and steel and textile industries without any real management reform or modernization of means of production. These industries were already looking out of date in 1914 when compared to foreign competition; by 1918 this situation had become worse and the industries were too large for peacetime needs. The country's transport system was overworked and, again, starved of the re-equipping it so badly needed. By 1918 British industry was not well placed to cope with ordinary times, yet the fact that Britain had won the war led to a shrinking from really bold reforms. Countries that had been defeated accepted massive change more readily; countries that had largely escaped serious involvement in the war were better placed in the struggle for trade. Britain, however, struggled to carry on in much the same way as before.

THE STATE OF SOCIETY

About forty-four million people lived in the United Kingdom in 1918. For those now returning from the fighting, and for those who had stayed at home the war had been a great disturber of previously accepted ways of living. Among many ordinary people there was a restless feeling that a better Britain must be built after so terrible a war, and that improved housing, education, pensions, etc. ought to come soon. Among ex-servicemen especially there were impatient

Returning servicemen hoped for great things from post war Britain

Q.M.A.A.C.'s being demobilized. War service did much to advance the cause of women's suffrage

desires to see change and a strong contempt for any attempts to deceive them.

The war had shaken up British society, forcing the well-to-do into closer proximity with ordinary people whether in trenches, on board warships or in factories producing the needs of war. Some middle-class people, disturbed by what they saw of the grim lives lived by ordinary folk in industrial towns, joined the recently formed Labour Party and looked to it for real social reforms. In any case the war had forced Britain's leaders to take more notice of the standard of living of working people. It needed the co-operation of workers to turn industry over to war production and this meant giving trade unions new respectability and importance. Army recruiting showed up the poor physical shape of the population. Many men were found to be suffering from the results of wretched food and diseases that could have been prevented had they been able to afford proper medical care. The low level of popular education was all too evident and forced the government to plan for improvements.

In some ways the war brought benefits to ordinary people. Although prices had shot up during the war and, at first, wages had lagged behind, by 1918 this lost ground had been made up and some workers were even slightly better off. The system of rationing brought in by the government had helped ordinary people obtain a better diet and more factories built canteens to provide an adequate midday meal for their workers. The weaknesses in health and education shown by the war led to a string of government schemes for reform, and this at a time when governments had more power to carry out change than ever before.

The position of women was clearly changed by 1918. Mrs Emily Pankhurst's suffragettes, who had been demanding that women be given the vote, turned instead, once the war broke out, to demanding 'the right to serve'. Some joined the army's new women's military corps and drove lorries and ambulances; others worked on buses or in factories. Middle-class ladies were at last introduced to the harsh life of everyday work in industry, and factory owners were forced to see how their premises must look to their new recruits. So important a contribution to the war effort could not be ignored and a new Parliamentary Reform Act in 1918 gave the vote to women over 30 as well as to all men over 21. It is true that women were still not being treated equally. A niggling property qualification remained in that land to the annual value of £5 must be owned or occupied by women or their husbands. But women were allowed to become M.P.s and the sting was completely taken from the suffragette movement. The change in their importance led to greater displays of independence by women. Their skirts were shorter, they smoked, they went out without male escorts.

These changes were examples of a greater loosening of old traditions and restrictions. Workers in towns had never been great church-goers but after 1918 attendance at churches fell even further. Instead people seemed to prefer to go to cinemas, sports stadia, or dance halls. A war in which so many had died and others had lived in such misery seemed to produce a mood in 1918 in which immediate pleasures mattered more and rapid social changes were expected. It was up to the wartime coalition government led by Lloyd George to show what it could offer the voters.

THE STATE OF POLITICS

When the Great War began H. H. Asquith led a Liberal government which, together with Labour and Irish Nationalist support, had kept the Conservatives in opposition for nine years. The Great War ruined the massive Liberal Party. Its principles of peace abroad, low taxes, free trade, and very limited interference in people's lives made little sense in wartime. Asquith went into a physical decline and his attempts to run the war on Liberal principles led to growing

Documentary One

The end of the War

So that night it was impossible to drive through Trafalgar Square; because the crowd danced under lights turned up for the first time for four years. A long nightmare was over; and there were many soldiers, sailors and airmen in the crowd which, sometimes joining up, linking hands, dashed like the waves of the sea against the sides of the square . . . it was deliverance from mud and poison gas, from night patrols and No Man's Land, and going over the top, from tetanus, tanks and shell fire, from frost and snow and sudden death. To their dung-coloured world of khaki in sodden trenches it seemed until today as if the politicians had clamped them for ever.

From LAUGHTER IN THE NEXT ROOM by Osbert Sitwell, 1949
Reprinted by permission of Macmillan, London and Basingstoke

The new Parliament viewed by a journalist

Coalitionists overflowed three quarters of the chamber occupying not only the ministerial side, but also the benches below the Opposition gangway, where formerly the Irish party had been predominant. Linked only by recognition of the Prime Minister's services in the war, the huge majority suffered for a time from its very bigness and from its limited sense of political discipline.

From FROM GLADSTONE TO LLOYD GEORGE by A. Mackintosh, 1919

The Prime Minister, as seen by the Secretary to the Cabinet

In stature Lloyd George was rather small, but he possessed the stocky solid frame of many of his fellow countrymen, and his healthy complexion gave evidence of a sound constitution. His head was square and large with a wealth of black hair gradually turned grey by the cares of Office. The dominating feature of his face was his eyes, ever changing; eyes astute, unfathomable. And from the man there emanated an extra-ordinary sense of power and strength.

From THE SUPREME COMMAND by Lord Hankey, 1961
Reprinted by permission of 2nd Baron Hankey

The Prime Minister, as seen by his Private Secretary

He was capable of immense and continuous application and never seemed to be bowed down by the strain of work or the press of events. The more desperate the situation, the more buoyant and resilient he became.

He could sleep at will, and when possible he snatched a short sleep after lunch. He went to bed early, usually at ten, threw off the problems of the day and read himself to sleep with a wild west adventure story. He woke early—soon after six, and read the pile of papers and memoranda which his secretaries had left by his bedside.

From LET CANDLES BE BROUGHT IN by Sir Geoffrey Shakespeare, 1949
Reprinted by permission of Macdonald and Jane's

THE PEACE TREATIES

The problems facing Lloyd George's peacetime ministry were almost as difficult to deal with as the problems of wartime had been. Whilst Germany was still being blockaded to make sure that it did not revive before its future was settled, the leaders of the victorious allies gathered in Paris to settle the fate of Germany, Austria, Hungary, Turkey and Bulgaria. Many of the ministry's supporters still felt great anger against Germany for the war that had just ended and expected to see a peace treaty that dealt harshly with her. Lloyd George, however, feared that a badly-treated Germany would remain bitter, eager for revenge and a possible prey for a Communist takeover. Communists controlled the Russian government and were very active in Hungary and Germany; the setting up of a sound, prosperous, democratic Germany seemed to the British Prime Minister to be a way of keeping Communists at bay.

But Lloyd George was not simply thinking of Europe's future; he made equally sure that wider British interests were protected. The Treaty of Versailles that eventually decided Germany's fate forced Germany to hand over her battle fleet to Britain and to agree to very severe restrictions on future warship building whilst totally banning submarines. Germany's overseas colonies were taken from her and, though there were supposed to be all sorts of checks and controls on how new colonies were run, in fact they were handed over to Germany's recent enemies and, especially, to the British Empire and Dominions. With Britain protected from German naval and colonial rivalry, it seemed to Lloyd George to be safe to work for a Continental Germany that was not treated too harshly.

His views clashed with those of Clemenceau, the French leader. After two wars in which France had suffered a great deal, Clemenceau was determined to see Germany so permanently crippled that she could never strike at France again. Germany's army was limited to 100,000 men and denied tanks whilst the German Rhineland (on France's border) was to be a wholly non-military area even after allied troops ended their fifteen years of occupation. Small areas were taken from Germany and handed to Belgium and Denmark; France recovered Alsace-Lorraine which she had lost in 1871; the Saar industries were to be run for France's benefit. Lloyd George felt some doubts over settling these western frontiers of Germany—especially over an unsuccessful French scheme to separate the Rhineland as an independent state—but it was over Eastern Europe that he clashed most vigorously with Clemenceau.

In Eastern Europe, Poland was re-created from lands taken from defeated Germany and Austria, and from Communist Russia. France supported a powerful Poland as a further way of keeping the new Germany weak, and sought to extend Polish frontiers to a degree that Lloyd George thought unacceptable. Over the rich province of Silesia there was a particularly lively quarrel, but in the event Lloyd George did manage to shield Germany from the full fury of the French. Indeed his moderation alarmed some M.P.s and he received an anxious telegram urging him to stand firm and deal brutally with Germany.

There was further debate over what fines should be imposed on Germany once the allies had justified this by writing into the Treaty a clause attributing the whole blame for the war to the Germans. France saw the imposing of a huge debt as a way of keeping Germany weak, as well as of gaining compensation; but Lloyd George was torn between trying to secure compensation for Britain and keeping the 'reparations' (as the fine was called) to a size small enough for Germany to feel she could make the repayments. No satisfactory solution was found by Lloyd George since the French refused to reduce their demands. That they resented his attitude was not surprising for they hoped at least for firm military guarantees from Britain and the U.S.A. since several of their other demands had not been met. But when the U.S.A. Congress refused to ratify the Treaty of Versailles, Britain would not accept any obligation to France and the French felt cheated.

The Austrian Empire had collapsed at the end of the war and settling the terms simply involved recognizing the independent countries that emerged. The Turkish Empire roused more British interest since parts of it spread close to the Suez Canal—the vital route to India. Turkey itself was very severely reduced in size and

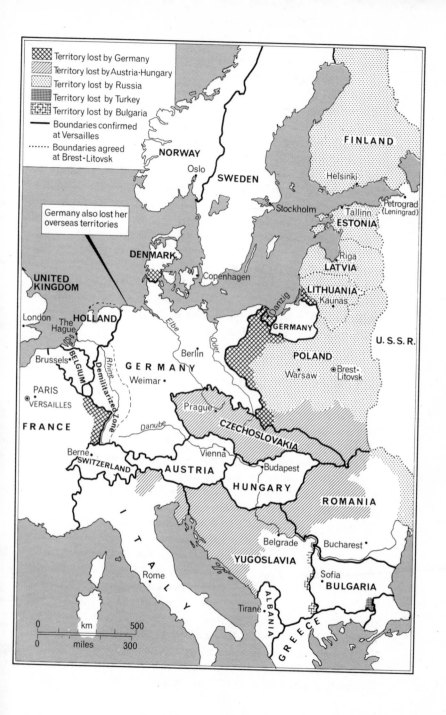

Territory lost by Germany
Territory lost by Austria-Hungary
Territory lost by Russia
Territory lost by Turkey
Territory lost by Bulgaria
Boundaries confirmed at Versailles
Boundaries agreed at Brest-Litovsk

Germany also lost her overseas territories

NORWAY
Oslo
SWEDEN
Stockholm
FINLAND
Helsinki
Petrograd (Leningrad)
Tallinn
ESTONIA
Riga
LATVIA
LITHUANIA
Kaunas
DENMARK
Copenhagen
UNITED KINGDOM
London
The Hague
HOLLAND
Brussels
BELGIUM
Elbe
Oder
Danzig
GERMANY
Berlin
POLAND
Warsaw
Brest-Litovsk
U.S.S.R.
PARIS
VERSAILLES
Demilitarized Zone
Rhine
GERMANY
Weimar
FRANCE
Prague
CZECHOSLOVAKIA
Berne
SWITZERLAND
Danube
Vienna
AUSTRIA
Budapest
HUNGARY
ROMANIA
ITALY
Rome
Belgrade
YUGOSLAVIA
Bucharest
Sofia
BULGARIA
Tirane
ALBANIA
GREECE

0   km   500
0   miles   300

Britain gained control of Iraq, Palestine and Transjordan from the wreck of the Turkish Empire.

The allies also agreed to the setting up of a League of Nations. This project was especially dear to Woodrow Wilson, President of the U.S.A., yet in the event the U.S.A. did not join it. The American Congress preferred to avoid becoming entangled in dangerous quarrels in Europe. Since the defeated powers of 1918 were left out and Russia was excluded, the League—intended as a means of solving future quarrels between nations peacefully—apparently became an organization in which the victorious powers made sure their enemies did not recover.

By 1920, fierce hatred of Germany was on the wane in Britain and Lloyd George was cheered by fellow M.P.s for the peace he had helped to negotiate. Yet it left huge problems—a bitter France, a resentful Germany and Turkey, Middle Eastern gains that soon proved to be troublespots and the question of reparations still not finally settled. Lloyd George was to find that the treaties by no means ended the need to deal with foreign crises.

LATER IMPERIAL AND FOREIGN AFFAIRS

Post-war Britain was faced not only with the cost of the conflict in terms of money, men and materials, but also with the growth abroad of a more powerful U.S.A. and Japan, with increasingly independent Dominions and with restlessness in many parts of the Empire. A vigorous foreign and imperial policy was more than Britain could now afford: she had to concentrate her efforts in very limited areas and seek to avoid expense elsewhere.

Lloyd George insisted on playing a major part in all aspects of affairs, and the mixture of negotiations in some areas and action in others was very much his policy. His attempt to hold conferences (for instance at Cannes and Genoa) in order to peacefully settle the question of money owed by various states to one another ended in failure. Britain had loaned her European allies more than she had received from the U.S.A. and was eager to see an agreement to cut or even scrap these debts. But the U.S.A. insisted on being repaid and France was bent on squeezing money out of Germany and not interested in schemes to end debts between countries. In the Washington Conference (1922) the Prime Minister's negotiations

Mahatma Gandhi as a young man

with other countries that had sizeable navies had more success, though it led policy in a way Lloyd George did not like. He favoured renewing Britain's alliance with Japan and dropped this reluctantly under pressure from the United States and Canada. At Washington the British agreed to battleships equal in number to the U.S.A.'s though more than those of Japan. Since Britain needed a strong navy in Europe this made her weak in the Far East and left her dependent on U.S. goodwill.

Britain's Empire was becoming less and less a source of military strength to her. Indeed in India, national leaders headed by Gandhi, began to make life difficult for the British forces as Indians pressed for a greater share in managing their affairs. The Montagu-Chelmsford Report (1918) proposed an Indian majority on the Legislative Council but did not really dent the power of the British Viceroy and his civil servants who kept control of justice, finance, the police and

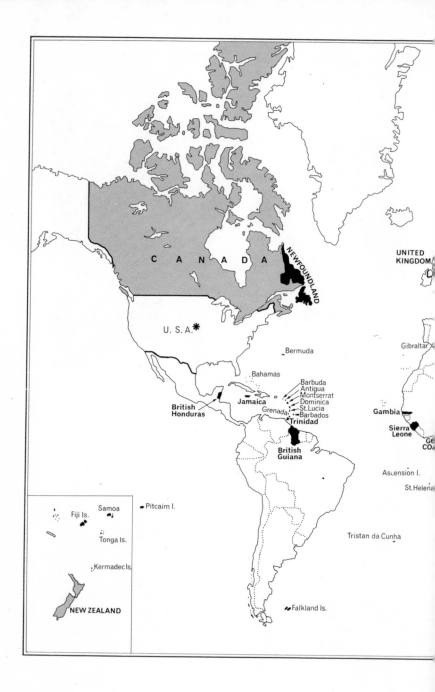

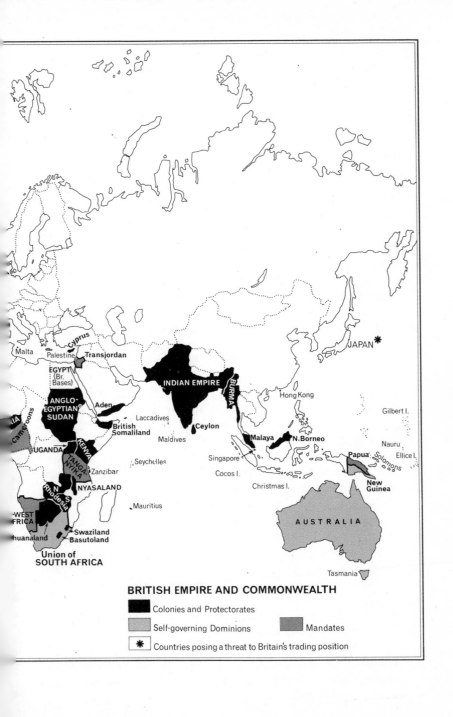

Malta Palestine Cyprus Transjordan

EGYPT
(Br.
Bases)

ANGLO-
EGYPTIAN Aden
SUDAN

Cameroons

UGANDA KENYA

British
Somaliland

Laccadives

INDIAN EMPIRE BURMA

Hong Kong

JAPAN ✳

Gilbert I.

Ceylon

Maldives

Zanzibar
TANGANYIKA

Seychelles

N. Rhodesia

NYASALAND

Mauritius

Cocos I.

Singapore

Malaya N.Borneo

Christmas I.

Nauru

Ellice I.

Solomons

Papua

New
Guinea

AUSTRALIA

WEST
FRICA

Bechuanaland

Swaziland
Basutoland

Union of
SOUTH AFRICA

Tasmania

BRITISH EMPIRE AND COMMONWEALTH

◼ Colonies and Protectorates

▨ Self-governing Dominions   ▨ Mandates

✳ Countries posing a threat to Britain's trading position

army. The result was ever larger protests until in April 1919 a large crowd of demonstrators at Amritsar met with gunfire from General Dyer's troops. 379 of them died and Gandhi replied by organizing disobedience to British rule. The Report's proposals were, none the less, embodied in the Government of India Act (1919). Nor were the new gains in the Middle East wholly a benefit. In 1917 the Balfour Declaration had committed Britain to providing a homeland for Jews in Palestine, and as Jews began to arrive, so a problem began to develop as Arab inhabitants became increasingly alarmed. In Egypt where British control had been present for longer, Egyptian nationalists were increasingly active, demanding that the British depart. But the Lloyd George government was determined to keep troops to secure British control of the Suez Canal and nothing they could offer, not even a kind of independence, satisfied Egyptians.

For some time after the end of the Great War, British troops continued to fight on the Continent though their enemy was Communist Russia not Germany. Troops who had originally gone in 1918 to protect supplies and try to replace the Communists with a government that would re-open the war with Germany, stayed on to help anti-Communist 'White' forces. Lloyd George felt increasingly unhappy about this policy that was so popular with anti-Communists in his Cabinet, especially Winston Churchill. He was eventually able to pull out British troops in 1920, arguing that Britain could not afford to be involved and that foreign troops only encouraged patriotic Russians to support the Communists. Nor was Lloyd George as eager as the French to help the Polish Army attack the U.S.S.R. in 1920. The limited military supplies gathered in Britain never even left home, for dockers refused to load the arms-ship, the *Jolly George*, and the T.U.C. threatened wider strikes.

Against such cautious policies, however, Lloyd George's Turkish policy stood out in contrast. He became heavily involved in helping Greece secure for herself a part of the mainland of Turkey and showed signs of a readiness to take risks that many of his colleagues found very alarming. The harsh terms forced upon Turkey in the Treaty of Sèvres caused so much anger that Turks overthrew their Sultan and set up in his place a Republic led by Mustapha Kemal. Turkish forces drove back the Greeks, chasing them steadily out of Asia Minor until they came face to face with British troops at Chanak. Only New Zealand was prepared to back Lloyd George's firm stand; other Dominions and France and Italy kept out of the crisis. General Harington at Chanak avoided clashing with the Turks and wisely failed to hand over Lloyd George's ultimatum to the Turks to withdraw. A new treaty, the Treaty of Lausanne, had eventually to be accepted in 1923 giving back to Turkey Istanbul as well as Asia Minor's Western coast. By then Lloyd George had lost office, a fall in which the Chanak crisis played an important part.

THE ATTEMPT AT SOCIAL REFORM

The misery of the Great War made many Britons determined to see a better homeland come out of it. During the war the government had used huge powers to raise money, control trade, organize transport, some industry and labour, and ration food. With powers like this, the ministry could do much more in peacetime than any earlier government had done. Moreover, Lloyd George still had a reputation as a reformer, had spoken in his election speeches of building 'homes fit for heroes' and, before the war had ended, had set up a Ministry of Reconstruction under Christopher Addison to plan for peacetime.

Yet shortly after the war was over there were widespread strikes and demonstrations, fuel shortages and a terrible flu epidemic that killed 150,000 people. A bitter anti-government feeling swelled up, even in the army where there were mutinies in protest at the way demobilization was proceeding. Winston Churchill acted to solve this problem, but it was less easy to solve the industrial crises. Trade unions were bigger and more respectable than before, for the war had led to their leaders working with the government and had encouraged small unions to merge together. The government feared a Communist revolution and treated some strikes too vigorously. On Clydeside came the most violent of clashes and the Clydeside leaders, Shinwell and Gallacher, were put in prison.

Though Lloyd George dealt with domestic problems when he could, foreign affairs took up much of his time and more conservative men dealt with day-to-day matters. Leaders of business and finance as well as many Conservative politicians wanted wartime taxes and controls done away with as soon as possible. Such men argued that Britain could not afford expensive welfare schemes, for the war had been so costly and the post-war boom in trade was very brief. The sudden end to the war had caught the ministry unpre-

The government hoped that this poster would pacify the miners

pared. Even if it had wanted to act vigorously, it had no detailed overall plan for prompt action to provide housing, better education and pensions, or to reorganize industry.

At least the troubles of 1919 seemed to fade in 1920. J. H. Thomas led the National Union of Railwaymen in a successful fight to stop wage cuts and Ernest Bevin managed to do the same for dockers. Miners' demands for shorter hours and more pay were put off by the appointment of Sir John Sankey to lead a commission to investigate the state of coal mining. The Commission's report favoured reduced hours and better conditions and, by one vote, nationalization too. However, the government shrank from this last step and merely reduced working hours in a day at the coalface to seven. Miners' anger was reduced by government help to allow a limited wage increase, but they remained far from satisfied.

Yet by the end of 1920 the ministry could point to some reforms. Christopher Addison became head of a new Ministry of Health and, as one of his duties, gave local authorities power and money to build houses for rent. In 1919 a Forestry Commission began to develop a timber industry in Britain; an electricity commission co-ordinated electricity production; through several industries groups of workers and management met to discuss the future of their industries. H. A. L. Fisher introduced a new Educational Act that raised the school leaving age to 14 and planned 'day continuation' schools so that part-time education for all children could continue up to 16 years. For those out of work, a new National Insurance Act (1920) extended the right to unemployment insurance to all lower paid workers except agricultural workers, civil servants and domestic servants. After they had made 12 contributions, unemployed men were entitled to fifteen shillings a week for 15 weeks in any year, and women to twelve shillings. This still left huge gaps, however, and was based on the belief that unemployment in Britain would affect only a small number of people.

In 1921 there came many signs of a drop in trade and business and a rise in unemployment, and the Lloyd George ministry promptly shrank back from the little in which it had become involved. Plans to electrify the railways were dropped and they were turned into four companies (in the war the state had run them); the mines were handed back to their owners who at once planned cuts in wages, longer hours, and different pay scales in different areas. The furious miners protested, were locked out by the owners, and appealed to

April 1921—coal strikers gather in Wigan market place

railwaymen and transport workers for help. But on a day that the miners called 'Black Friday', 15th April 1921, the other unions refused to help the miners and the three months' strike that followed ended in defeat for the miners. The Prime Minister now ridiculed Christopher Addison, forcing him to resign and killing off his housebuilding programme because it was far too costly. He appointed Sir Eric Geddes to find other ways of cutting government spending and accepted many of Geddes' suggestions such as cuts in teachers' salaries, the scrapping of day continuation schools, allowing huge classes in schools, cuts in armed forces' pay and in government contributions to the unemployment fund, and an end to child welfare and maternity benefits.

But the numbers of unemployed rose by July 1921 to two million and remained at a high figure. The Unemployment Fund soon spent all its money and the government had to bring in a new act in 1922. Now the ministry had to allow 'uncovenanted benefit', that is payments to the unemployed for which they had made no contribution when working. This payment soon became known as 'the dole' and still did not solve many problems. Not only was it tiny, but some groups of workers were left out, and for those involved in the scheme

The slump reduced many war veterans to selling in the streets

there was a gap between the end of unemployment insurance and the time when they received the dole. The local Poor Law Guardians raising money from the rates still had to provide help, and what they paid varied widely. The Labour Council of Poplar paid thirty-three shillings a week, but no other area paid so much and some would only help the unemployed if they went into work-houses.

By 1922 Lloyd George's election promises looked like a dreadful piece of deception and his claims to be a 'man of the people' had disappeared. The long shadow of unemployment cast across the lives of so many in the inter-war years had appeared.

THE IRISH PROBLEM

The outbreak of the Great War prevented the British government from giving Ireland the separate parliament to manage its own domestic affairs that so many Irish wanted. In the 1916 Easter Rising extreme nationalists made a vain attempt to seize Dublin and declare Ireland a republic, but the British government handled the affair so brutally that the numbers of nationalist supporters in Ireland rose rapidly. In the 1918 election, 73 seats were won by Sinn Fein, the party that stood for an independent Ireland. The new members refused to come to Westminster and instead set up their own parliament with De Valera as President and Michael Collins and Arthur Griffiths as leading ministers. To meet the expected British attack, Collins developed the Irish Republican Army and a network of spies.

To deal with what it saw as a rebellion, the Lloyd George ministry, urged on by many in the party who had long been against even home rule for Ireland, recruited ex-soldiers into the Auxiliaries and the 'Black and Tans'. These forces helped the Royal Irish Constabulary fight a savage war in which ambushes, terrorism, murder and destruction swept through the country. The Black and Tans (so named because of their black and khaki uniforms) were particularly unpopular and the whole war soon became the object of a Labour Party enquiry and press criticisms. The Irish problem was confused by the presence of a large Protestant group in Ulster totally opposed to Sinn Fein and fearful that in an independent united Ireland it would be swamped by the mass of Catholic votes.

Lloyd George offered Ireland two parliaments in the Government of Ireland Act, 1920. Ulster accepted and in 1921 George V opened

THE KINDEST CUT OF ALL.

Welsh Wizard. "I NOW PROCEED TO CUT THIS MAP INTO TWO PARTS AND PLACE THEM IN THE HAT. AFTER A SUITABLE INTERVAL THEY WILL BE FOUND TO HAVE COME TOGETHER OF THEIR OWN ACCORD—(ASIDE)—AT LEAST LET'S HOPE SO; I'VE NEVER DONE THIS TRICK BEFORE."

A hopeful Lloyd George—the trick does not seem to have worked yet !

its Parliament with a plea for an end to violence. But the rest of Ireland rejected the offer of a divided country and of control only of their own domestic affairs. Yet the war was costly to Irish nationalists too and, by late 1921, some at least were ready to negotiate. Michael Collins and Arthur Griffiths came to London and eventually agreed to a treaty on 5th December 1921. Lloyd George succeeded in outwitting them, suggesting a commission to draw the boundary between Ulster and the new Irish Free State that would make Ulster so tiny as to be unworkable and threatening total war if this were not accepted.

The treaty allowed British troops to leave Ireland, but enemies of the treaty continued to fight under De Valera's leadership and succeeded in killing Michael Collins. Eventually the government gained the upper hand, De Valera turned to politics, but the episode left most of Ireland far from grateful to Lloyd George and hostile to the parts of the treaty that retained British fleet bases in Ireland, and Ireland within the Commonwealth. Certainly the boundary commission did not cripple Ulster and was far from harsh to her frontiers.

THE DOWNFALL OF LLOYD GEORGE

By 1922 the huge majority that made up the coalition Lloyd George led was beginning to break up. The Prime Minister's Liberal followers felt especially bitter for he made no attempt to keep their loyalty and spent his time with men they did not like. The ideas they believed in seemed to mean little to Lloyd George: he used violence in Ireland, which they hated: he brought in the Safeguarding of Industries Act 1921 putting a $33\frac{1}{3}$ per cent duty on many imports, yet Liberals still believed in free trade. They replied by refusing to agree to his plans to merge them completely with the Conservatives—some of them even began to drift over to the Labour Party.

Among Conservatives there was just as much restlessness. Senior Cabinet ministers like Balfour and Austen Chamberlain were content to go on working with Lloyd George, but many back benchers and party workers saw no need of him now the war was over. The feeble coalition Liberal Party seemed to them to be merely a nuisance and they longed to see a wholly Conservative government instead. The

Chanak crisis increased their worry and brought open attacks from Lord Curzon, the harassed Foreign Secretary, and the former Conservative leader Bonar Law. Nor did Lloyd George do his reputation any good by the cheerful way he increased the 'Lloyd George Fund' by selling honours to men widely thought disreputable.

When news came that Lloyd George planned an election to be fought again by a coalition, there was a revolt among the Conservatives. On 19th October 1922, Conservative M.P.s met at the Carlton Club and voted by 187 to 87 to end the coalition. Speeches to them by senior ministers were heard in silence; it was Bonar Law and Stanley Baldwin who won applause for their belief in an end to coalition. Lloyd George had to resign and in an election in November Bonar Law led the Conservatives to a victory over Liberal and Labour parties. For Lloyd George this marked the end of his career in power, for not only did many Conservatives hate him and Labour suspect him, even his own Liberal Party distrusted a man who seemed ready to pick up and cast them aside when it suited him. Without a large party on which to build, Lloyd George was lost.

Documentary Two

A triumphant peace

Utterly broken in will and physical power, Germany, at 4.15 p.m. yesterday bowed to her crowning humiliation and accepted the peace imposed on her by the Allied Nations.

For Mr. Lloyd George, who signed for the British Empire, more, perhaps than for any other personage present, it was a day of extraordinary triumph.

His handiwork was complete when ratification took place. At that moment the new political map of the world came into effect and the magnificent German Empire of a few years ago stood stripped, formally, of some of her most treasured European provinces, of all her colonial possessions, of her Shining Sword, and her powerful navy.

From the NEWS OF THE WORLD 11th January 1920

Industrial differences widen

There were movements growing with demands for shorter working hours, more pay, and more power both over industry and in the government of the country.

Although there were many employers with vision, it cannot be said that the majority did more than comply with the bare necessities required by Factory Acts or interested themselves much in extra amenities, the housing of their workpeople or their social aims of all kinds. The tendency to widen the gulf of classes was rapidly making headway on both sides. There was not enough human relationship between leaders of industry and the rank and file, particularly the young men.

From INDUSTRIAL PROBLEMS AND DISPUTES, Lord Ashwith, Chief Industrial Commissioner at the Board of Trade 1920

Lloyd George no longer a man of the people

I notice that Lloyd George has steadily veered over to the Tory point of view. He constantly refers to the great services rendered by captains of industry and defends the propriety of the large share of the profits they have taken. He wants to improve the world and the condition of the people but wants to do it in his own way.

From INTIMATE DIARY OF THE PEACE CONFERENCE AND AFTER by Lord Riddell 27th March 1920

The unemployment problem

Mr. Clynes, addressing a Labour Meeting at Batley last night said no one desired acts of lawlessness, but the privations and bitter prospects were so terrible and so provoking that such acts should not surprise anybody.

There was not a more pathetic spectacle than the unemployed victims of our social order. They included a large number of men who a few years ago were priceless heroes, but who were now worthless wasters.

From the NOTTINGHAM JOURNAL 20th December 1920

In spite of the assistance given by the unemployment benefit and by outdoor relief, the physique of a great number of Manchester workers is undoubtedly being impaired by prolonged unemployment. That the majority of the unemployed are disheartened and miserable and feel utterly helpless and insecure, there can be no doubt.

From the report of an enquiry undertaken in the Autumn of 1922

Violence in Ireland

The Irish Republican Army did not hold the open field for an hour against 10,000 troops: they nevertheless succeeded in worrying an army of 110,000 out of the country. Battalions without end poured into the remotest villages without any visible resistance to their armoured cars and great artillery; but the practical results of their occupation vanished as promptly as the fortifications built by children on the foreshore.

From THE IRISH REVOLUTION AND HOW IT CAME ABOUT
by W. O'Brien 1923

A fresh outbreak of mob violence was witnessed in Belfast on Wednesday of last week. The attacks on Catholic shops and dwelling houses as well as on the Catholic residents then renewed, have continued into this week. No fewer than 25 fires were attended by the Fire Brigade.

From the IRISH WEEKLY INDEPENDENT, 4th September 1920

It is officially stated that at nine o'clock yesterday morning simultaneous attacks were made on military officers and ex-officers in their lodgings in various parts of Dublin. 14 persons in all appear to have been killed and 6 wounded. The auxiliary police captured 3 of the assassins.

Most of the men were killed in their bedrooms or in their beds and in one case an officer was shot in the presence of his wife.

From the MANCHESTER GUARDIAN 22nd November 1920

The Carlton Club meeting, 19th October 1922

At Chamberlain's entry there was little or no applause, while Balfour and Birkenhead took their seats amidst a chilly silence. Bonar Law on the other hand was greeted with a spontaneous outburst of clapping.

Chamberlain's speech was the reproof of a schoolmaster scolding an unruly class and when he claimed that there were no differences between the Conservatives and Lloyd George, there was a loud growl of dis- agreement.

From THE EMPIRE OF THE AIR 1957
by Viscount Templewood (Conservative M.P.)
Reprinted by permission of the Estate of Viscount Templewood

The Prime Minister was described this morning in The Times *in the words of a distinguished aristocrat as a 'live wire'. He was described to me and to others in more stately language by the Lord Chancellor as 'a dynamic force' and I accept these words. He is a dynamic force and it is from that very fact that our troubles in our opinion arise. A dynamic force is a very terrible thing; it may crush you but it is not necessarily right.*

It is owing to that dynamic force and that remarkable personality that the Liberal Party, to which he formerly belonged, has been smashed to pieces; and it is my firm conviction that, in time, the same thing will happen to our party.

From a speech made at the Carlton Club meeting
by Stanley Baldwin quoted in STANLEY BALDWIN by G. M. Young
Reprinted by permission of Granada Publishing Ltd.

THE PARTY'S RISE TO OFFICE

The Conservatives, who had thrown aside Lloyd George, won a comfortable victory in the November 1922 elections. The closest challenge to Bonar Law's Conservatives came from 142 Labour M.P.s for the divided Liberal Party managed to win only 117 seats altogether. Bonar Law was becoming progressively more ill from cancer, and in May 1923 he had to retire. With so many leading Conservatives still linked to the name of Lloyd George, the man they had wanted to continue to cling to in 1922, the way was clear for Stanley Baldwin to become Prime Minister.

Baldwin's political career had been fairly brief and not very impressive when compared to coalition supporters like Austen Chamberlain. But his only rival in 1923 was Lord Curzon. Curzon was not very popular and many thought it unwise to have, as Prime Minister, a member of the House of Lords—hence the success of Stanley Baldwin. A government with 347 seats seemed in no danger, yet in eight months it had gone. Baldwin felt that the troubled question of unemployment might best be solved by switching to a policy of large-scale duties on foreign imports; he decided that he needed the country's support before risking this step.

In fact in November 1923 the British rejected what Baldwin offered them. Both wings of the Liberal party were able to come together in defence of free trade and secured 159 seats. Labour did even better, winning 191 seats and, like the Liberals, sharply criticizing Baldwin's plans for protection. This meant that, though there were 258 Conservative M.P.s, the government was defeated in important votes in the Commons by the combined Liberal and Labour M.P.s. Thus to the great surprise of the Labour Party they were rapidly catapulted into power. In January 1924, King George V sent for their leader, Ramsay MacDonald, and asked him to form a government.

MacDonald (Prime Minister), Thomas (Colonial Secretary), Henderson (Home Secretary) and Clynes (Lord Privy Seal) leave the palace after a Privy Council meeting

THE NEW GOVERNMENT

Ramsay MacDonald was a distinguished looking man with a long record of Labour Party service as a leader and as a writer, and with considerable ability as a public speaker. Yet he had never been in a government before and he was only now in office as a result of the Liberals' decision to give Labour their support. He managed to be popular both with moderate Labour men and with the left wing who wanted bolder policies and who were rather deceived by MacDonald's attacks on the Great War into thinking he agreed with them. He had to struggle to hold together a party that was a very recent creation and which was still very much an alliance of trade unionists, socialists and the intellectual middle-class moderates of the Fabian Society.

The Prime Minister completed his Cabinet by appointing men who were very recent converts from Liberalism, the most important being Lord Haldane and Charles Trevelyan. Only two of his ministry—Haldane (Lord Chancellor) and Arthur Henderson (the Home Secretary) had ever held Cabinet office before. Most of the ministry—including MacDonald himself and his Chancellor of the Exchequer, Philip Snowden—were working-class in background, very ignorant of the ways of government, and had to lean heavily on the advice of their civil servants. Despite the fact that 136 of the Labour M.P.s were trade unionists, few unionists got office. Only one key post went to a man with any claims to being a left winger—the Ministry of Health which was given to John Wheatley.

MacDonald tried to hold together a party quite unused to office by using the powers of the Prime Minister very vigorously. This at once raised the question in the minds of Labour men as to whether MacDonald was betraying the party. It was only in 1918 that Labour had obtained a national organization, and the party represented a new background and approach. Its party executive was elected by an annual conference and there was some feeling that MacDonald should take his orders from the party conference. The party's 1918 programme, 'Labour and the New Social Order', drawn up by Sidney Webb, had been vague, but it had included the famous *clause four* which suggested Labour believed in nationalization. Thus, before he ever seriously grappled with detailed policies MacDonald was in trouble in trying to find a competent government (by drawing on ex-Liberals) and in using all the powers of the Prime Minister's office. Both these factors offended men who had helped form the Labour Party and wanted to see Socialists in office who took their guidance from the party conference.

Philip Snowden

ECONOMIC AND SOCIAL POLICIES

MacDonald and Snowden wholly rejected the suggestion of some left wingers that the government should at once introduce socialist measures, even if this did mean the Liberals would turn against them. The party had no detailed socialist programme to put into operation and its leaders were determined to prove they were a respectable body of men fit to rule Britain. MacDonald's speeches sounded impressive yet they were very vague, whilst Snowden was better at delivering biting attacks on enemies than in producing clear policies of his own.

A big reform programme to tackle all the social problems Lloyd George had begun to struggle with before the slump would have been expensive, and expensive plans repeatedly failed to get past the Chancellor of the Exchequer. Philip Snowden seemed to believe that the nation should pay its way in the same careful and austere fashion that he ran his own life. Far from agreeing to increased expenditure he became as strong a believer in cutting taxes as any Liberal. He halved import duties on tea, sugar, cocoa and coffee; he swept away the import duties created during the war by the Liberal McKenna; he abolished a profits tax on corporations. Most Labour men knew little of economics and found it impossible to stand up against Philip Snowden.

John Wheatley's housebuilding programme was one of the few reforms to pass Snowden—and then probably because the cost was

The new housing estates epitomized people's hopes of a better, peaceful and more prosperous future

spread over so many future years. Wheatley came from the Clyde-side, a region which persistently produced many left wing Labour men, and the success of this owlish bespectacled figure was rather a surprise to contemporaries. He reorganized and extended earlier attempts by Addison and Chamberlain to encourage housebuilding by providing a £9 million subsidy to make local authorities build council houses for rent. His schemes did not help the poor, but they did lead to the eventual building of half a million homes for the more prosperous members of the working-class.

Trevelyan, President of the Board of Education, met with a degree of success, too, with policies that were not immediately

New schools and smaller classes greatly advanced education

costly. He increased free places in secondary schools, restored University state scholarships that the Geddes axe had abolished, and worked for the reduction of school classes to a maximum of forty pupils. The Hadow Committee that he appointed produced proposals in 1926, for a leaving age of 15 and a switch from primary to secondary schools at 11, that were to have a big effect on later policy.

But the problem of unemployment baffled the ministry. It spent £28 million on public works but was basically opposed to this kind of solution. Old age pensions and unemployment benefits were both improved, but this was merely tinkering with the system. As later years were to show, Labour had nothing to offer as a clear, serious, and well thought-out plan for tackling unemployment.

INDUSTRIAL UNREST

Almost immediately after its election, the Labour government found itself faced with a wave of strikes, and in particular with strikes involving Ernest Bevin's Transport Workers. A ten-day strike by dockers for two shillings a day closed every port and brought victory for the strikers—who rejected government offers to mediate. Strikes by tram and bus workers, shipyard workers and railway shop workers added to government feelings that there was a crisis. Despite the fact that the Labour Party leaned heavily on trade unions for support, the government took emergency powers for itself. Though these powers were not used, the fact that a Labour ministry was ready to use troops against trade unionists was a further dent in the image of the party leaders as Socialists.

WORLD AFFAIRS

Ramsay MacDonald acted as his own Foreign Secretary. He enjoyed the world of international affairs in which he now moved and was especially successful as chairman of conferences. He had always been more interested in foreign affairs than most Labour men and he clearly cared about putting Britain at the head of the struggle to create a peaceful world where quarrels were solved by discussion.

The League of Nations: internal discord and the lack of American support doomed it to failure from the beginning

MacDonald was the only British Prime Minister ever to attend the League of Nations. Like the rest of his party he had overcome early doubts about the League and put a lot of his time into trying to make it flourish. He was helped by the rise to power in Europe of two other moderates ready to co-operate in a bid at peaceful problem solving—Herriot in France and Stresemann in Germany. With both countries British relations improved and MacDonald's work helped to smooth relations between France and Germany too. French troops left the Ruhr—which they had seized to try to squeeze from the German economy the reparations Germany would not pay. Above all, MacDonald played a big part in getting all concerned to agree to a new attempt at solving the reparations problem—the Dawes Plan. The Dawes Plan seemed to produce annual reparations Germany was ready to pay and France to accept; in fact it depended on U.S. loans to Germany, but for the moment this did not seem a weakness.

MacDonald had less success with an attempt to give the League more power to force trouble-making countries to accept its decisions. This scheme—the Geneva Protocol—was killed off by MacDonald's Conservative successors, but MacDonald himself appeared very hesitant about it once it seemed likely to be accepted generally. He also faced critics who felt he should not be accepting reparations at all, nor should he be appearing to suggest to France that a Labour Britain accepted the Versailles Treaty.

The ministry also attempted to improve British relations with Russia. Some Labour men felt great sympathy with Communist Russia, some felt better relations might mean improved trade for Britain, and all were agreed that Russia should not be treated as an outsider in Europe. The government gave official recognition to Russia's Communist government and worked on plans for treaties to improve trade and financial arrangements between the two countries.

But towards the Empire MacDonald and his Colonial Secretary, J. H. Thomas, proved very reluctant to be bold. Thomas spoke of the Empire with pride, sent the R.A.F. to bomb tribesmen in rebellion in Iraq, and refused to agree to Egyptian demands that Britain should pull out of the Suez Canal area and the Sudan. Spending on the navy dropped as a cruiser building programme was cut from eight to five vessels and work on the Singapore base stopped; but spending on the R.A.F. went up.

THE FALL OF THE GOVERNMENT

Much to the irritation of the Liberals, the Labour Government made no effort at all to behave in a polite and considerate manner towards those whose votes it needed. Lloyd George in particular became angry about this and looked for a chance to launch an attack on MacDonald's government. Labour's Russian policy offered just such an opportunity and a clash threatened over the government's decision to offer Russia a loan in return for Russian repayment, in part at least, of British assets in Russia that had been seized.

But the actual break with the Liberals came over the Campbell case. Conservatives and Liberals joined together to denounce and defeat the government when it decided to drop the charges it had considered bringing against a Communist journalist, J. R. Campbell. One of Campbell's articles in the *Workers' Weekly* urged British soldiers not to shoot at fellow workers and the Attorney-General had him charged for incitement to mutiny. The case was soon dropped as being a foolish fuss over words many Labour men had used from time to time, but the Conservatives insisted that this meant altering the course of justice as a result of political pressure. A vote of censure was passed by 364 to 191 and MacDonald called a general election for October 1924.

THE ELECTION

The mild and moderate Labour ministry members found themselves fighting a very emotional campaign in which their opponents attacked the Labour leaders as the friends and allies of Communism. It was not surprising, then, that a considerable fuss should have been caused by the publication, five days before polling day, of a letter from a Russian leader urging Communists to work for Labour's treaties with Russia as a step towards revolution in Britain. This 'Zinoviev Letter' has remained a mystery. The original has never been produced, the letter was published by civil servants without MacDonald's permission (he was on an election tour) along with a letter of protest MacDonald had drawn up to be used if the Zinoviev Letter proved genuine. It may well have been a forgery, but it was published by men arguing that the government should release it before the *Daily Mail*, which also had a copy, could do so.

In fact it may not have made all that much difference to the result, for Labour's poll went up, even though its number of M.P.s dropped to 151. The Liberals suffered most, for without the free trade issue and facing a reunited Conservative Party, they were cut down to 42 members. This left 419 Conservatives in an overwhelmingly powerful position to take power again under Baldwin.

The Zinoviev Letter did help MacDonald to stay at the head of his party. He was able to claim that Labour was tricked out of office and his left wing critics, led by James Maxton, found their attacks on the party leadership for being far too cautious were easily beaten off. Labour remained a very moderate party of reform led by the same men as in 1924. Communists were held firmly at arm's length; Labour would not join the Russian-led Communist International organization; the leadership would not accept I.L.P. plans for bolder reforms at home. Instead Labour waited behind MacDonald's powerful but vague screen of speeches until power would slip, inevitably, to it. No detailed policy planning went on. Labour had no intentions of doing anything that was dramatic.

The claim that Zinoviev's 'real' name was 'Apfelbaum' was designed to suggest that, as well as being a Bolshevik, he was also a German Jew

MOSCOW ORDERS TO OUR REDS.

GREAT PLOT DISCLOSED YESTERDAY.

"PARALYSE THE ARMY AND NAVY."

AND MR. MACDONALD WOULD LEND RUSSIA OUR MONEY!

DOCUMENT ISSUED BY FOREIGN OFFICE

AFTER "DAILY MAIL" HAD SPREAD THE NEWS.

A "very secret" letter of instruction from Moscow, which we publish below, discloses a great Bolshevik plot to paralyse the British Army and Navy and to plunge the country into civil war.

The letter is addressed by the Bolsheviks of Moscow to the Soviet Government's servants in Great Britain, the Communist Party, who in turn are the masters of Mr. Ramsay MacDonald's Government, which has signed a treaty with Moscow whereby the Soviet is to be guaranteed a "loan" of millions of British money.

The letter is signed by Zinoviev, the Dictator of Petrograd, President of the Third (Moscow) International, and is addressed to A. McManus, the British representative on the executive of this International, who returned from Moscow to London on October 18 to take part in the general election campaign.

Our information is that official copies of the letter, which is dated September 15, were delivered to the Foreign Secretary, Mr. Ramsay MacDonald, and the Home Secretary, Mr. Arthur Henderson, immediately after it was received some weeks ago. On Wednesday afternoon copies were officially circulated by the Executive authorities to high officers of the Army and Navy.

A copy of the document came into the possession of *The Daily Mail*, and we felt it our duty to make it public. We circulated printed copies to other London morning newspapers yesterday afternoon. Later on the Foreign Office decided to issue it, together with a protest, dated yesterday, which the British Government has sent to M. Rakovski, the Bolshevik Chargé d'Affaires in London.

The salient passages of Moscow's plot letter are:

Armed warfare must be preceded by a struggle against the inclinations to compromise which are embedded among the majority of British workmen, against the ideas of evolution and peaceful extermination of capitalism.

Only then will it be possible to count on complete success of an armed insurrection.

From your last report it is evident that agitation-propaganda work in the Army is weak and the Navy a very little better. . . . It would be desirable to have [propaganda-agitation] cells in all the units of the troops, among factories working on munitions and at military store depots.

The military section of the British Communist Party further suffers from a lack of specialists, the future directors of the British Red Army . . . . . It is time you thought of forming such a group.

The British protest is signed, in the absence of the Foreign Secretary, Mr. MacDonald, by Mr. J. D. Gregory, Permanent Assistant Secretary of the Foreign Office. It requests a reply "without delay."

The text of this protest is in another column

Zinoviev, whose real name is Apfelbaum.

FOREIGN OFFICE PROTEST.

REPLY WITHOUT DELAY REQUESTED.

The following is the text of the letter sent yesterday by Mr. J. D. Gregory to M. Rakovski, the Chargé d'Affaires in London of the Soviet Union:—

FOREIGN OFFICE,
October 24, 1924.

Sir,—I have the honour to invite your attention to the enclosed copy of a letter which has been received by the Central Committee of the British Communist Party from the president of the Executive Committee of the Communist International, over the signature of Member Zinoviev, its president, dated September 15.

The letter contains instructions to British subjects to work for the violent overthrow of existing institutions in this country, and for the subversion of his Majesty's armed forces as a means to that end.

2. It is my duty to inform you that his Majesty's Government cannot allow this propaganda and must regard it as a direct interference from outside in British domestic affairs.

3. No one who understands the constitution and the relationships of the Communist International will doubt its intimate connection and contact with the Soviet Government. No Government will ever tolerate an arrangement with a foreign Government by which the latter is in formal diplomatic relations of a correct kind with it, while at the same time a propagandist body organically connected with that foreign Government encourages and even orders subjects of the former to plot and plan revolutions for its overthrow.

Such conduct is not only a grave departure from the rules of international comity, but a violation of specific and solemn undertakings repeatedly given to his Majesty's Government.

4. So recently as June 4 of last year the Soviet Government made the following solemn agreement with his Majesty's Government:—

The Soviet Government undertakes not to support with funds or in any other form persons or bodies or agencies or institutions whose aim is to spread discontent or to foment rebellion in any part of the British Empire . . . and to impress upon its officers and officials the full and continuous observance of these conditions.

5. Moreover, in the Treaty which his Majesty's Government recently concluded with your Government, still further provision was made by the faithful execution of an analogous undertaking which is essential to the existence of good and friendly relations between the two countries.

His Majesty's Government mean that these undertakings shall be carried out, both in the letter and in the spirit, and it cannot accept the contention that while the Soviet Government undertakes obligations, a political body, as powerful as itself, is to be allowed to conduct a propaganda and support it with money, which is in direct violation of the official agreement.

The Soviet Government, either has or has not the power to make such agreements. If it has the power then it is its duty to carry them out and see that the other parties are not deceived. If it has not then its power and its responsibilities which belong to the State in other countries are in Russia in the keeping of private and irresponsible bodies the Soviet Government ought not to make agreements which it knows it cannot carry out.

6. I should be obliged if you would be good enough to let me have the observations of your Government on this subject without delay.

I have the honour to be,
with high consideration, Sir,
Your Obedient Servant,
(in the absence of the Secretary of State)
(Sd.) J. D. GREGORY.

M. C. Rakovski,
Etc., etc., etc.

Documentary Three

Extract from the Labour Party's 1918 Constitution

Party Objects.

[a] To organize and maintain in Parliament and in the country a Political Labour Party, and to ensure the establishment of a local Labour Party in every County Constituency and every Parliamentary Borough;

[b] To co-operate with the Parliamentary Committee of the Trades Union Congress, or other kindred Organizations, in joint political or other action in harmony with the Party Constitution and Standing Orders;

[c] To give effect as far as may be practicable to the principles from time to time approved by the Party Conference;

[d] To secure for the producers by hand or by brain the full fruits of their industry, and the most equitable distribution thereof that may be possible, upon the basis of the common ownership of the means of production and the best obtainable system of popular administration and control of each industry or service.

Sidney Webb

Ramsay MacDonald

The Prime Minister's behaviour in Cabinet was perfect. He was never discourteous, never overbearing, never unduly dogmatic, patient to everyone, watchful to give everyone a chance to speak . . . I think that the rest of us also behaved well. We certainly never quarrelled, never wrangled with each other.

From THE FIRST LABOUR GOVERNMENT BY Sidney Webb

The new Labour Government's problems

The Labour Party was composed in the majority of new and undisciplined members who would expect the Labour Government to do all sorts of impossible things . . .

There would be two courses open to us. We might use the opportunity for a demonstration and introduce some bold Socialist measures, knowing, of course, that we should be defeated upon them. Then we could go to

*the country with this illustration of what we would do if we had a
Socialist majority. This was a course which had been urged by the
extreme wing of the Party, but it was not a policy which commended
itself to reasonable opinion. I urged very strongly . . . that we should
not adopt an extreme policy, but should confine our legislative proposals
to measures that we were likely to be able to carry . . . We must show
the country that we were not under domination of the wild men.*

From AN AUTOBIOGRAPHY Vol. II, by Philip Snowden, (1934)

Part of the Zinoviev Letter

*It is indispensable to stir up the masses of the British proletariat to
bring into movement the army of unemployed proletarians whose
position can be improved only after a loan has been granted to the
USSR. . . . A settlement of relations between the two countries will
assist in the revolutionising of the international and British proletariat
. . . the establishment of close contact between the British and Russian
proletariat, the exchange of delegations and workers, etc., will make it
possible for us to extend and develop the propaganda of ideas of Leninism
in England and the Colonies . . .*

*With Communist Greetings
President of the Presidium of the IKKI
Zinoviev.*

STANLEY BALDWIN

In 1924 Stanley Baldwin was fifty-seven years old and for the next ten years was to hold more power for longer than anyone else in British politics in the inter-war years. He looked a calm, pleasant, honest and trustworthy man—indeed the large sums he gave to charity are examples of his concern for others. At the end of the Great War his worry about the size of Britain's debts was such that he gave £120,000 (one-fifth of his estate) to the Treasury. In fact the Prime Minister was far more sensitive, tense and emotional than his outward appearance suggested. He suffered from bouts of nervous exhaustion and found it difficult to concentrate on details of government to the extent that some fellow ministers thought him lazy.

But Baldwin possessed qualities that seemed to suit his times. After the bold but risky policies of Lloyd George, Baldwin seemed honest and reliable. If he offered little but vague promises of goodwill to voters, this seemed to be what many of them wanted. He had a most effective manner of speaking; simple, direct and unaffected that contrasted strongly with the speaking style of Lloyd George or

Mr and Mrs Baldwin, at the time of his retirement from politics

Winston Churchill. In 1924 Baldwin used radio broadcasts to the nation in his election campaign and at once proved more successful than his rivals. According to one contemporary Mrs Baldwin sat knitting quietly by his side whilst her husband chatted to the nation.

Baldwin had spent much of his life running the family's iron works, yet his love of the English countryside was strong and pictures of him in rural surroundings may have helped spread the image of the pipe-smoking, true Englishman whom people could trust.

THE NEW GOVERNMENT

Baldwin had not been a very effective Opposition leader. He found it difficult to launch fierce attacks on Labour: indeed he even allowed his party whips to help the inexperienced Labour men. Yet he had done much to pull his party together after the 1922 crisis, and he had improved its organization. His 1923 election campaign did not go well, yet by declaring for protection he had won back pro-Lloyd George Conservatives like Austen Chamberlain who believed in this kind of policy. By then dropping this policy and seeming to stand firm against Socialism, others—like Winston Churchill—rallied to the Conservative cause. He had reorganized the party's headquarters, helped by Neville Chamberlain, and had set up a proper Shadow Cabinet.

Baldwin's quiet personality and rather lazy ways may have annoyed men eager for action, but did help him hold together a government with many very different and very determined personalities. Austen Chamberlain became Foreign Secretary and his younger half-brother Neville, Minister of Health. Lord Birkenhead took charge of Indian affairs and that recent convert from Liberalism, Winston Churchill, became Chancellor of the Exchequer. To please his party's right wing, Baldwin appointed as Home Secretary the violently anti-Communist William Joynson Hicks. 'Jix', as he came to be known, was a determined hunter of Reds: he prosecuted 12 leading Communists and allowed a police raid on the Soviet trading organization in London. But he had his supporters in the party and on prison reform was very enlightened.

Baldwin himself provided an image for the party that made it seem sympathetic to ordinary people. He spent a great deal of his time in Parliament, talked frequently with ordinary M.P.s, and made a very favourable impression on his Labour opponents. His speeches were usually well received—one speech in 1925 in which he pleaded for an end to bitterness between different groups in society and ended with the cry 'Give us peace in our time, O Lord' received a very warm and emotional response.

DOMESTIC REFORMS

Unlike Lloyd George, Baldwin really believed in allowing his ministers to run their departments. His government was responsible for a number of social reforms and the key figures in carrying them out were Winston Churchill and Neville Chamberlain. Churchill was no expert financier, but Baldwin thought him too dangerous to leave out of office. His policy reflected what his civil servants and advisers thought best and, oddly for a man who was later to make so much fuss about rearmament, he concentrated on cutting spending on the armed forces. It was Churchill who insisted that policy be based on the principle that there would be no war involving Britain for at least ten years. He reduced income tax to four shillings, restored the McKenna import duties that Snowden had scrapped, and worked with Chamberlain on various reforms.

Neville Chamberlain was just the kind of conscientious, hard-working minister that Baldwin needed. He could master all the complicated details that Baldwin could not be bothered with, and during this ministry he guided twenty-one bills through Parliament. Chamberlain liked to see government working efficiently and his reforms were aimed at this goal. In the course of this period he did help the lives of quite a large section of the population, yet somehow he always seemed too cold and distant to gain popular recognition.

In general, government policy led to an increase in government power. Conservatives might attack Labour's Socialism, yet they helped subsidize Imperial Airways, they created the B.B.C. as a public corporation and they passed the Electricity Supply Act of 1926. The latter bill created a Board appointed by the Minister of Transport which brought power from generating stations and distributed it to private or municipal electricity supply companies. The Conservatives also extended the right to vote. In 1928 women were given the vote on exactly the same terms as men. Moreover,

Chamberlain continued the policy of providing local authorities with subsidies for building council houses for rent. It was under him that the bulk of the half a million houses Wheatley worked for were actually built.

In 1925 Chamberlain introduced a new pensions bill. A basic ten shillings a week pension was provided for those over 65 covered by the Health Insurance scheme; widows were entitled to a ten shillings a week pension and orphans to seven shillings and sixpence. People who were outside the scheme were less well treated, though, and those who were ill suffered very variably. Insured employees could obtain free treatment yet, strictly speaking, their dependants could not. The insurance was in the hands of a number of companies and some were more generous than others; some men's record of ill-health was such that no company would take them and a local Insurance Committee had to ensure they obtained treatment.

The persistent problem of unemployment forced Chamberlain into action. He did not like the way local poor law guardians could use rates in methods that varied from region to region, and in 1926 obtained power to over-rule any guardians who defied what the minister thought to be right. After the Blanesburgh Committee had looked at the unemployment insurance problem in 1927, Chamberlain cut both contributions and benefits. Though he did widen the scope of benefits there were still many not covered by insurance at all.

In 1929 he carried out a major reform that, in part, was to tackle the chaos of unemployment relief. The old Poor Law Unions were finally scrapped and instead the duty of helping poor people not covered by insurance fell upon the much bigger counties and county boroughs. Their Public Assistance Committees had much larger regions to look after than the bodies they replaced which helped them spread the burden of cost more fairly. They were given a government grant, based on the needs and population of each area and for poorer regions this helped shift some of the cost from the ratepayer to the government. The act also helped agriculture and industry by freeing the former from rates and by making the latter liable for only one-quarter of their rates burden. Neville Chamberlain made the existing system work more efficiently and fairly: but he and his fellow Ministers would do nothing really bold to help the unemployed.

THE GENERAL STRIKE 1926

British industries continued to struggle to compete in world markets and to find employment for people at home. Churchill did not make things any easier, in 1925, by restoring the gold standard with the pound at £1=$4.86. This over-valued British currency made it even more difficult for British exports to sell since it raised their prices.

At the centre of the troubled industrial scene stood the coal industry. It was out of date—there were over 1,400 separate mining companies—it was badly run, and it was faced with the competition of foreign coal that was cheaper, and with the growth of other sources of power. Mine owners answered this problem by attempting to reduce wages, pay different wages in different regions, and extend hours of work. Miners refused to accept such terms and Baldwin was only able to prevent a crisis in 1925 by giving a nine-month subsidy that would make wage cuts unnecessary for the moment.

He appointed Sir Herbert Samuel to lead a commission to look at the coal industry, and in March 1926 this Commission (consisting of men with no previous knowledge of the coal industry) offered solutions that neither miners nor owners would accept. Owners disliked the Commission's statements about the need to reorganize the industry totally, provide better conditions and set up a national wages board. Miners opposed the Commission's attack on government subsidies and on the need—temporarily at least—for there to be wage cuts.

The cause of the miners raised wide union support and brought the T.U.C. to the miners' aid. The moderate men who led the T.U.C. hoped this would make possible an end to the crisis by means of discussion. But Baldwin seemed to have little effect on the owners

Baldwin endeavoured to keep the peace between miners and owners

General Strike: a volunteer drives a bus under police escort

and his own party included men who urged him to fight the coal miners. During the temporary peace brought by the subsidy, the government had taken care to organize the country into ten regions and to allow a volunteer organization for the Maintenance of Supplies to grow up; the T.U.C. had done nothing to prepare for battle.

On 1st May the miners struck and the T.U.C., having failed to negotiate a settlement with the government, called out other unions in support. Baldwin's behaviour seemed odd. He used the excuse of the *Daily Mail* printers refusing to produce a leading article attacking the strike to break off negotiations, yet the T.U.C. was in no way responsible for this episode. At midnight on 3rd May, other unions also came out on strike with very impressive solidarity. Yet though 2½ million men had stopped work, union funds were not up to a long battle and most of their leaders were not eager for such a clash. The government had volunteer help to run road and rail transport and used troops to protect the movement of supplies from the docks.

Despite the violent attacks on strikers by the *British Gazette*—run by Winston Churchill—the actual intentions of strikers were moderate. When Herbert Samuel produced a scheme suggesting how his report might work, T.U.C. leaders grasped at it as a reason for ending the strike even though miners rejected it and the government would make no promises. Officially at least the strike was over by 13th May, though when workers realized what was happening a new, brief, but much more bitter unofficial strike occurred. The miners themselves stayed out till December when hunger and misery forced them to give in and accept the owners' terms. Union membership and affiliations to the T.U.C. fell and the ministry drove home its victory with the Trade Disputes Act which declared general strikes illegal, banned civil servants from joining the T.U.C., and made union men who wished to subscribe to the Labour Party pay in quite separately instead of automatically contributing as part of their union subscription.

The strike damaged the leadership of more extreme unionists like A. J. Cook, the miners' secretary. The T.U.C. was now led by Walter Citrine and Ernest Bevin, men who favoured progress by working through the Labour Party.

SOCIAL LIFE IN THE TWENTIES

Though a million and a half men were out of work at this time, others were on strike and many people lived grim lives, for the well-to-do the pace of social life gave the period the name of 'roaring twenties'. The desire to forget the past war and present

The inhuman working conditions in the mines continued for many years after the 1926 failure

troubles may have helped create the hectic social life of the fashionable young that is described in the novels of Aldous Huxley and Evelyn Waugh. The much freer and more independent position of women may also have had something to do with it. Certainly their short hair, short skirts, boyish fashions and cigarette-smoking seemed part of a general attempt to show that women were liberated at last. In 1919 Lady Astor became the first woman M.P.; many legal barriers to women entering certain careers were scrapped; in 1923 the Matrimonial Causes Act allowed women to sue for divorce on the grounds of adultery.

Fashionable life consisted of rounds of cocktail parties and balls, and dancing some of the fashionable dance crazes like the Charleston to jazz bands. A crowded social calendar included Henley, Ascot, Wimbledon and holidays abroad. Some churchmen, facing falling church attendances, vigorously criticized what they saw as falling moral standards among Britain's young.

Ordinary people who could hold on to their jobs found that, in many ways, they too were better off. Real wages went up and hours were reduced, giving a margin of money and time to spend. Some of this money went on the growing number of items mass-produced

Whatever the economic ills, crowds still flocked to Wimbledon

THE SWING OF THE PENDULUM.

THAT THE TWENTIETH-CENTURY GIRL,—

AFTER HAVING BOBBED HER HAIR—

THEN SHINGLED IT—

THEN ADOPTED THE ETON CROP—

NEVER QUITE REACHED THE DARTMOOR SHAVE—

AND IS NOW STARTING TO GROW IT (AND HER DRESS) AGAIN.

How Punch *saw the fashion scene*

by industry and sold by large stores like Woolworths. Some went on a better diet—in 1929 Seebohm Rowntree found 6·8 per cent of York's population living in dire poverty compared to 15·46 per cent in 1899.

Money was also increasingly spent on travel. Railway trips were now supplemented by bus outings. The 1920's were the heyday of the tram, yet the appearance of the bus marked the eventual downfall of the tram. Manchester was the first big city to start replacing trams with buses, for buses could cover greater distances, use different routes, link up villages and towns and take people on long outings. Whereas motor cars had once been a means of travel for the rich, prices fell in post-war years to bring them within reach of the middle-classes. In 1922 the inexpensive Austin 7 was produced and by 1928 a Morris Minor cost a mere £125. As there was no driving test, anyone over 17 could drive a car. By 1930 when Britain contained over a million cars the maximum speed limit—20 m.p.h.—was scrapped. Motor cycles numbered 720,000 in 1930 and many working-men owned bicycles.

Morris Minor   *A petrol station*

Popular entertainments also expanded. Sport became more and more organized for spectators—cricket, greyhound racing and, perhaps most of all, soccer. Wembley Stadium opened in 1923 for a cup final between Bolton Wanderers and West Ham. George V presented the cup to Bolton, the winning side. Newspapers and magazines and especially the *Daily Express*, the *Daily Mail* and the T.U.C.'s *Daily Herald*, fought for popular attention.

The 1920's saw a big growth in cinema attendance and the building of huge and elaborate palaces to which people could go to forget their troubles, surrounded by luxury, and view films that almost certainly came from Hollywood. From 1926 onwards the silent film rapidly disappeared before the onslaught of the 'talkies'. Romantic figures like Rudolph Valentino, Douglas Fairbanks and Gloria Swanson gave ordinary folk someone with whom to identify to escape their own existences.

In the early twentieth century the wireless was developed. Other countries were quicker than Britain to see the entertainment value of this invention, but the *Daily Mail*'s paying for Dame Nellie Melba

Marconi sits amongst his equipment
(inset) a balanced crystal set

to sing for half an hour seemed to work something of a change in 1920. A British Broadcasting Company of 1922 was turned into a public corporation in 1926. Its head was John Reith, a Scotsman who insisted on high moral standards and the use of radio for improving the nation's tastes in music and literature. He insisted that his announcers wear evening dress.

In many ways life in Britain in the 1920's was more decent and pleasant than in earlier years. Diet improved, more houses had baths, clothing improved, drunkenness decreased. More people had holidays, more people travelled. But very little was done for education or health by the government and in Scotland, South Wales and the north of England the presence of large numbers of men unable to find work brought bitterness and despair. Life was still very hard for working people, but at least there were signs of improvements from pre-war days.

Documentary Four

The Prime Minister's views on industrial relations given in the House of Commons on 6th March 1925

Suspicion which has prevented stability in Europe is the one poison that is preventing stability at home, and we offer the country today this; we at any rate are not going to fire the first shot. We stand for peace. We stand for the removal of suspicion in the country. We want to create an atmosphere, a new atmosphere in a new Parliament for a new age, in which the people can come together.

Two views on the General Strike

Everyone must realise that, so far as the General Strike is concerned, there can be no compromise of any kind. Either the country will break the General Strike or the General Strike will break the country.

Not only is the prosperity of the country gravely injured, not only is the immense and increasing loss and suffering inflicted upon the whole mass of the people; but the foundations of the lawful constitution of Great Britain are assailed. From the BRITISH GAZETTE 7th May 1926

The General Council does not challenge the Constitution. It is not seeking to substitute un-constitutional government. Nor is it desirous of undermining our Parliamentary Institutions.

The sole aim of the Council is to secure for the miners a decent standard of life. From the BRITISH WORKER 7th May 1926

The cinema

They first walked through an enormous entrance hall, richly tricked out in chocolate and gold, illuminated by a huge central candelabra, a vast bunch of russet gold globes. Footmen in chocolate and gold waved them towards the two great marble balustrades, the wide staircase lit with more russet globes, the prodigiously thick and opulent chocolate carpets, into which their feet sank as if they were the feet of archdukes and duchesses. . . . It was an interval between pictures. Several searchlights were focused on an organ-keyboard that looked like a tiny gilded box, far below, and the organ itself was shaking out cascades of treacly sound, so that the whole place trembled with sugary ecstasies.

From ANGEL PAVEMENT by J. B. Priestley
Reprinted by permission of William Heinemann Ltd.

GENERAL ECONOMIC DIFFICULTIES

The high unemployment and low export figures after 1918 owed something to the Great War but had their roots in nineteenth-century history. Britain's industrial revolution of the late eighteenth and early nineteenth centuries had given her a big lead over other nations in the production of coal, iron and steel, textiles, and heavy engineering goods. With British products in demand all over the world, British trade and shipbuilding had flourished. Other countries had resources of coal and iron and possessed skilful workmen and prosperous agriculture, but Britain had enjoyed more peace at home than her rivals. Her government had not hindered economic changes and transport of heavy goods was made easy by sea, navigable rivers and canals.

In the later nineteenth century this situation began to change as other individuals and other governments saw the power and riches brought by industrial growth. Railways (pioneered in Britain) helped other countries by offering a fast, cheap and reliable way of moving heavy goods in areas without water transport. By 1914 Britain was facing challenges to her leadership of the first industrial revolution. At the forefront of this challenge were the U.S.A. and Germany and

An industrial skyline

not far behind were Japan and France. Britain's rivals seemed more ready to accept new methods of production of coal, steel and textiles, and they were more open to new ideas than British industrialists who often preferred to trust what had served them well in the past.

Britain's major industries after 1918 were still these basic industries and they all depended heavily on exports. In 1914, 75 per cent of cotton production was exported and over 100 million tons of coal were sent abroad in 1913. Post-war years showed how the challenge of foreign competition had harmed Britain. Except for 1923, only in good years did coal exports reach 50 million tons: other countries could produce coal more efficiently, and electricity and oil challenged coal's lead as a provider of energy. Iron and steel, shipbuilding, textiles and heavy engineering all struggled with the same problem. All leaned heavily on exports yet all were faced with fierce foreign competition and with new rival products.

In the later nineteenth century a kind of second industrial revolution had developed on electrical and chemical industries, plastics, light engineering and the internal combustion engine. These developments usually needed plenty of money and teams of highly trained scientists, yet Britain still preferred to trust in the practical craftsman and in on-the-job training. Far too little was spent on scientific and technical education and in these newer industries Britain lagged well behind her main rivals in 1914.

British governments in the nineteenth century had swept away import and export duties in order that Britain could obtain food and raw materials for industry very cheaply whilst exporting the products of British industry at low cost. This had greatly harmed agriculture which could not compete with cheap food from the spacious areas of North America, Russia, and Australia and New Zealand. Other countries—such as Germany—protected their farmers: many British farmers were ruined. The free-trade policy also meant that the products of foreign industry could easily enter British markets. Although the Great War had seen a change of policy here, by the 1920's British agriculture and industry were once again struggling to compete even at home with very little protection from their own government.

Only the briefest of booms had followed the Great War. Thereafter Britain settled into a slump in which exports were too low, new industries too small and there seemed to be a permanent pool of well over one million unemployed.

The long queue of unemployed wait outside the Labour Exchange

THE COMING OF THE GREAT DEPRESSION

Between 1924 and 1929 the U.S.A., Germany, France, and many other countries enjoyed a boom that was denied Britain. The boom depended heavily on credit and especially on United States loans and in 1929 it began to collapse. In late October 1929, panic selling of stocks and shares developed in Wall Street, New York. The boom of the previous years had not been healthy—shares had risen to very high levels and the whole apparent prosperity rested more on credit than on real industrial and social improvements. Once confidence began to wobble it proved hard to stop a collapse as people rushed to sell shares and withdraw savings. Banks and companies failed, trade and production shrank, and unemployment rose. Americans understandably stopped lending abroad, called in their loans, and the crisis spread to Europe.

The situation was made worse by the fact that by 1929 many countries that relied chiefly on producing food and raw materials found that they were marketing more than they could sell. The value of these 'primary' products therefore fell, leaving the food-producing countries less able to purchase the exports of manufacturing nations such as Britain. All this helped diminish world trade and placed further barriers before British producers in the shape of foreign import duties imposed by governments trying to protect their own floundering economies.

THE SECOND LABOUR GOVERNMENT

In the 1929 general election the problems of unemployment and the economy played a large part. The boldest policies were offered to the voters by Lloyd George's Liberals who claimed, 'We can conquer unemployment'. Lloyd George had dipped into his considerable funds to run a genuinely national campaign based on policies that had been thoroughly worked out by teams of experts from politics, finance, industry and intellectual life. Their programme of public works to provide jobs and improve Britain depended on higher taxes and government borrowing. Both of the other parties rejected it almost completely. Over five million votes went to the Liberals but the mere 59 M.P.s that resulted from all this effort was an acute disappointment to their leader. The policies he had worked out were too detailed for most voters to understand, his promises were distrusted after 1918, and his party organization was in poor shape.

David Low cleverly depicts the problems faced by the second Labour government which had neither majority nor policy

Margaret Bondfield

Most voters—over 17 million—clearly preferred the vague and cautious policies of the Labour and Conservative parties. There was enough irritation with Baldwin for the vote to be split roughly equally between the two parties, the result being the election of 288 Labour and 260 Conservative M.P.s. The outcome was a Labour Government—led once more by MacDonald, Snowden, Henderson and Thomas—that had no clear majority. Probably this made little difference; these men had no plans for bold reforms, and they kept left wingers out of important office though they did give Britain her first woman Cabinet minister—Margaret Bondfield, Minister of Labour.

Labour made life for those in need slightly less harsh. They improved unemployment benefits, cut miners' daily hours of work from eight to seven and a half. Christopher Addison set up marketing boards to control sales and prices for different branches of agriculture and Arthur Greenwood not only continued subsidized house building but began a slum clearance programme as well. To do more than this demanded more planning and determination than Labour men could offer. In any case there was little time, for the effects of the world depression began to spread to Britain.

LABOUR AND THE GREAT DEPRESSION

Since Britain had not shared in the boom of the 1920's, the Great Depression seemed less savage in Britain than in the United States and Germany. British banks were sufficiently large and skilful to avoid the collapses that were common in other parts of the world. Yet between 1929 and 1931 British exports fell rapidly to about half their previous volume and the bulk of these exports were the products of the old industries that were already in trouble. As a result unemployment figures climbed from 1·2 million in mid 1929 to $2\frac{1}{2}$ million in late 1930.

MacDonald's reaction was to set up a special committee under the leadership of J. H. Thomas. One member of the committee who had very radical ideas was Oswald Mosley, Chancellor of the Duchy of Lancaster, who drew up a Memorandum on the economic crisis that he put before the Cabinet and the party. Both rejected it and Mosley despaired of ever seeing bold solutions come from ordinary British political parties. He left the Labour Party, followed by four other M.P.s, and set up the New Party. However, he soon became so impressed by Mussolini and Fascism that he lost support of former

Oswald Mosley receives the Fascist salute from his followers

colleagues. His party became Britain's version of Fascism but was never a powerful mass movement.

Mosley's Memorandum advocated tariffs on imports, public control of banking, the development of agriculture, more pensions and allowances and the reorganization of industry. Like Lloyd George's 1929 proposals, these reforms would have been costly and Mosley believed that the government would have to borrow heavily. Countries as different as Fascist Italy and the parliamentary democracy of Sweden followed this kind of policy and it was also a policy being vigorously pushed by a number of men in Britain. The most important of these men was the economist John Maynard Keynes, who had already made a name for himself by his attacks on the Versailles Treaty and on Churchill's restoration of the gold standard. He had helped Lloyd George with his 1929 policies and was soon to launch a book which had a dramatic and lasting impact on national economics and the outlook of statesmen and politicians. Keynes believed that a crisis like that of 1929 should be met by governments spending more and not, like Philip Snowden, trying to balance budgets. Increasing taxes and borrowing heavily would make possible a programme of public works that would provide more jobs and give these employees a purchasing power that would, in turn, keep others in employment too.

But the ideas of Keynes, Lloyd George, Mosley and anyone else who suggested heavy spending repelled Philip Snowden, his Treasury advisers, and many City financiers. Inter-war Britain was not a country ready to take risks and the ministry reflected this.

THE DOWNFALL OF LABOUR

Since Mosley's ideas had been turned down and J. H. Thomas had little to offer, MacDonald took control of the economic crisis and put Sir George May in charge of a committee to suggest action. The May Report of 31st July 1931 put the gloomiest possible interpretation on the situation, predicted a huge government deficit in the next year and declared that taxes should be raised by £24 million a year. Like Geddes, under Lloyd George, May also demanded huge economies totalling £96 million. The salaries of teachers, civil servants, police and the armed forces were to be reduced, but the bulk of the cuts were to fall on the unemployed whose benefits were to be slashed by 20 per cent.

The May Report appeared at a very unfortunate time. Opinion was already worried by that part of the Macmillan Report on Finance and Industry that had pointed out that what Britain actually exported did not equal in value what she imported. In fact this had been true for a century and the gap was usually more than covered by earnings from banking, shipping, insurance and overseas investments, but it had never really registered so strongly before. Moreover, in late July gold was flooding out of Britain at the rate of £2½ million a day as Britain paid for staying on the gold standard with small reserves and an over-valued currency. To meet the crisis, loans from Paris and New York were arranged and it seemed to the government that the loans would only be forthcoming if Britain carried out severe economies.

Pay cuts were accepted by the Cabinet but reduction of unemployment benefits (even when brought down to 10 per cent) was more than many members of the government could accept and aroused furious opposition from the T.U.C. It seemed clear that the government was going to fall. George V called the party leaders together and put to them the idea of a coalition suggested by Sir Herbert Samuel (who was leading the Liberals in the absence, through ill health, of Lloyd George). The Prime Minister, Thomas and Snowden and a handful of Labour M.P.s accepted this idea but the bulk of the party rejected it. On 24th August 1931 the Labour government ended in a bitter mood with sharp attacks being launched at the former leadership.

In October 1931 MacDonald called an election asking the country for 'a doctor's mandate' to deal with unemployment. 556 coalition men were elected whilst George Lansbury led a mere 46 Labour M.P.s. Though Labour attacked MacDonald as a traitor and Snowden called Labour ideas 'Bolshevism run mad' there was not a great deal of difference between them in terms of actual policies. The weakened Labour Party depended heavily on the T.U.C. for support in this crisis and continued to reject bold reforms offered by men like Stafford Cripps. MacDonald's ministry was dominated by 471 Conservative M.P.s. For the moment, as in 1918, they were prepared to accept the leadership of a man from another party provided he could help Britain emerge from the crisis.

Documentary Five

The causes of depression

There is first, the class of industry which is still suffering from a wartime expansion in excess of normal peacetime requirements ... In this class fall iron and steel, shipbuilding and certain branches of engineering, and to some extent, coalmining. There is second, the class of industry that before the war was dependent to a great extent on exports, and that has suffered since the war a loss of part of its overseas market, coupled in some cases with an invasion by imports of its home market.

Report of the Royal Commission on Unemployment Insurance 1931-2
Reprinted by permission of HMSO

Sir Oswald Mosley's suggestions, given in the House of Commons on 28th May 1930

We have to face up to the fact, that if men are to be employed on any large scale that employment has to be paid for either by the State or by local authorities ... Further, it must be remembered that to set many men working for a year costs a great deal of money ... It must be raised by loan ... This money, under a three-year programme, would be raised as and when required to pay for that programme over a period of three years. It is not a question of raising £100,000,000 right away ...

Why is it so right and proper and desirable that capital should go overseas to equip factories to compete against us, to build roads and railways in the Argentine or in Timbuctoo, to provide employment for the people in those countries while it is supposed to shake the whole basis of our financial strength if anyone dares to suggest that raising of money by the Government of this country to provide employment for the people of this country?

Philip Snowden's policy upsets the Labour Party

Its effect on the Labour members was stunning. They regarded this as the end of their hopes that the Labour Government would proceed with a policy of spending public money on extravagant schemes of social reform ... The Left Wing members of the Labour Party at once began to express their dissatisfaction and disgust with the statement. One of them declared: 'It's bigger, not smaller budgets we want'. They showed not the

least appreciation of the national situation, nor of the fact that the de-
cline in revenue and in trade made it impossible to carry out a policy of
increased expenditure which might have been possible when trade was
booming and revenue expanding.

From AN AUTOBIOGRAPHY by Philip Snowden 1934

The end of the second Labour Government

At 2.30 the Cabinet Room is crowded. All Ministers not in the Cabinet,
and all Whips, are invited. J. R. M. sits alone on the other side of the
long table . . . He had originally summoned us, he says, to tell us that our
salaries were to be cut. But now he has to tell us that the Government is
at an end. He is very sorry. We shall curse him and he is afraid he has
caused us great embarrassment. . . . He has not called us here in order to
form any cave, or to ask us to join him. He realises that he is committing
political suicide.

From CALL BACK YESTERDAY by Hugh Dalton
Reprinted by permission of Frederick Muller Ltd.

THE COALITION GOVERNMENT

Conservative strength was shown in the post-election government by the appointment of Neville Chamberlain to the key post of Chancellor of the Exchequer. Baldwin, as Lord President of the Council, acted as a kind of deputy prime minister until June 1935 when he replaced MacDonald (whom ill health forced to resign). The 35 National Liberals led by Sir John Simon (who became Foreign Secretary) agreed with the Conservatives on so many issues that it was hard to tell them apart. MacDonald's 13 National Labour supporters were too few in number to make much impact on policy and the rest of the Liberals (33 in all) also lacked strength. In 1932 these Liberals, and Philip Snowden, resigned from the coalition leaving Conservatives even more clearly in charge.

The Cabinet of the National government. Left to right: (back row) Cunliffe Lister, Thomas, Reading, Chamberlain, Hoare; (front row) Snowden, Baldwin, MacDonald, Samuel, Sankey

But Baldwin's grip on his party was not very secure. He was criticized for fighting a rather feeble election campaign in 1929: the right wing of his party rallied to Winston Churchill's leadership in attacks on Baldwin for supporting the Labour policy in India of giving more control over affairs to Indians themselves.

Above all Baldwin faced a national attack mounted by Lord Beaverbrook and Lord Rothermere who used their control over the *Daily Express*, the *Evening Standard*, the *Daily Mail*, and the *Daily Mirror* to attack the Conservative leader. Beaverbrook even set up a separate political group in 1930, the United Empire Party, and challenged an official Conservative candidate with a candidate of his own in a 1931 Westminster by-election.

Not only did Beaverbrook dislike Baldwin personally, he believed the policies he offered were feeble. Beaverbrook's answer to Britain's troubles was to draw together Empire and Commonwealth in a much closer relationship. He wanted the government to put taxes on foreign food imports, leave imperial products untaxed, and thus develop an imperial free trade area. Though Baldwin was not against tariffs, he was roused to effort by this challenge to his leadership. In a fierce speech to his party he denounced the press lords for exercising 'power without responsibility'. His party remained loyal to him and Duff Cooper, the candidate who supported Baldwin in the Westminster by-election, defeated the United Empire Party's challenge.

COALITION ECONOMIC POLICIES

The replacement of Labour by a coalition in itself seemed to calm the City. The cuts that had worried Labour were carried out by the coalition, though a mutiny by 12,000 sailors at Invergordon enabled the navy to escape pay reductions. Income tax was raised, contributions to unemployment benefit were put up, government aid to housebuilding was stopped, adding up to a bleak series of policies that at least pleased financiers.

There were other financial changes too, not least the abandoning of the gold standard. In 1932 by the Exchange Equalization Act the Treasury set aside £150 million to draw on for dealing with any sudden rush of financial speculation. Negotiations with the U.S.A. and France led to a 1936 agreement that none of the three countries would alter their exchange rates without consulting the others. The government cut the cost of the Debt by lowering bank rate from 6 per cent to 2 per cent in 1931-2. Though this made money cheaper to borrow the government itself kept a very tight hand on loans.

These were all very much the policies of Neville Chamberlain who seemed to flourish in times that needed tough measures. He restored the cuts in unemployment benefit in 1934 and reformed the control of unemployment by an act that put management of relief in the hands of a public Unemployment Assistance Board. This improved efficiency, but the Board paid relief according to rigid scales that were lower than rates paid by some local authority assistance committees. Even more important, the Board insisted that the whole family of someone asking for unemployment relief should have their income examined by a searching means test.

But the introduction of tariffs was, perhaps, the most striking of the coalition's actions. At last, in peacetime, Britain dropped free trade. A hasty, temporary power to put duties of up to 100 per cent on items coming into Britain in abnormal quantities was followed by a more careful measure in 1932. Duties of between 20 per cent and 30 per cent were put on imports with the exception of a number of foods and raw materials, together with imperial imports that were left for discussion later in the year. In July 1932 at Ottawa, representatives of Britain and her Empire and Commonwealth found that reaching agreements about trade was very difficult. So much of the Empire had built up its own industries and trade with countries other than Britain that free trade was quite unacceptable. Britain had to make do with duties on her manufactured exports to the Empire at a lower rate than those on the exports of other countries, and in return she gave preference to imperial butter, fruit, cheese and wheat.

The slump forced even a Conservative dominated government to intervene more vigorously in economic affairs. The creation in 1931 of B.O.A.C. from a merger of two airways looked very much like a kind of nationalization, whilst in 1935 help to housebuilding emerged again, though this time the emphasis was on clearing slums. By 1936 government help to British agriculture by subsidies totalled £40 million, and the various marketing boards were encouraged to grade and price their products for what was becoming a guaranteed market. The government encouraged reorganization in coal, iron and steel, textiles and shipbuilding with a view to scrapping inefficient works, helping the more efficient, and to the creation of bigger units of production. In shipping, for instance, there was a subsidy for building tramp shipping and favourable loans to owners who would scrap out-of-date vessels and order new ones. But help for areas in distress was small. The two commissioners who were appointed to develop regions that were suffering most had spent little over £2 million (by 1939) on new industries; that sum created less than 50,000 new jobs. From 1935 onwards rearmament resulted in spending that often helped depressed industries but this was spending the government resented. Basically the coalition believed in restoring confidence by balanced budgets whilst doing what was necessary to protect Britain's economy from being a dumping ground for the surpluses of other lands.

ECONOMIC RECOVERY

After reaching 2·8 million in 1932, unemployment figures fell below 2 million in 1936 and then stuck at around 1·5 million. Government policy may have had some effect, yet tariffs were too low to permanently counter foreign competition and may have done no more than halt a further slide. The Ottawa agreements probably diverted to the Empire some trade that might have gone elsewhere rather than increasing the volume of trade. Cheap money helped firms and individuals to borrow more easily; the government itself continued to keep a tight hand on loans. Spending on defence rose from 10 per cent

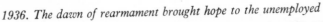

1936. The dawn of rearmament brought hope to the unemployed

of government expenditure in 1934 to 30 per cent by 1939 and certainly helped iron and steel, aircraft, arms and shipbuilding. But though it helped the economy, rearmament forced the government into public spending that it did not really want.

Yet the economy did partially recover in the 1930's. Exports did not do particularly well, and their recovery was not very significant; it was at home that signs of improvement were clearest. Fortunately for Britain the size of her import bill fell drastically so that 1936 imports, though equal in volume to those of 1929, cost 32 per cent less. Thus people in work were better off and their ability to buy more with the same money helped the growth of British industries and steadied her now heavily subsidized agriculture. One of the earliest signs of recovery was a boom in private housebuilding from 1932, financed largely by building societies, and this encouraged the purchase of all sorts of items for the new homes.

Britain's industries benefited from the fact that, at last, British investors put their capital much more heavily in the domestic economy rather than sending it abroad. Both industry and agriculture spent more on research and on new machinery. Moreover Britain's newer industries did not lean so heavily on exports as to be badly hurt by the depression. In leather, paper and printing there was really no sign of depression. The production of electrical goods expanded and in the world of chemicals, the big firms, I.C.I., Unilever, Courtaulds and British Celanese, produced increasing quantities of plastics, chemicals, dyes, fertilizers, soap, medicines and synthetic fibres. Between 1929 and 1937 the number of cars exported by this expanding industry increased $2\frac{1}{4}$ times; yet the industry was supplying a growing home demand too. Thus industries with a firm base of domestic sales could do well in the 1930's; export-based industries continued to struggle and $1\frac{1}{2}$ million men remained out of work. It seems that Britain was fortunate that events worked in her favour to enable her to ride the depression as well as she did, for government, City, and civil service seem to have learned little from the crisis.

THE DEPRESSED REGIONS

Those parts of the country already suffering from the unemployment that resulted from dependence upon struggling industries found themselves even worse off after 1929. Basically these areas were near

The Jarrow marchers tramp their way to London

coal and iron fields, the areas of South Wales, Southern Scotland, North-east England and much of the North West and West Riding of Yorkshire. The level of unemployment in Jarrow reached 67·8 per cent of the labour force in 1934. In Merthyr Tydfil it was 61·9 per cent. In 1935 17 of the 33 coal pits in Bishop Auckland were abandoned, 3 more closed, and the rest worked small and irregular shifts. Iron and steel areas recovered better than those devoted to coal or ship-building—indeed new steel works were built in Ebbw Vale and Corby and in textiles cotton areas suffered more than the less export-dependent woollen industry. In many rural areas (like the Highlands and Islands of Scotland) there was great poverty. In Lancashire, the city of Manchester had enough industries other than cotton to suffer less than Oldham or Burnley.

Yet this still left huge regions of Britain living in conditions that seemed permanently miserable. It is not surprising that there were marches in protest—the most famous being the 1936 march by Jarrow men protesting that their town had been murdered by the death of its shipbuilding industry. An area with struggling industries suffered in other ways too. Men out of work for long periods often sank into apathy; their wives had to face a constant struggle to manage the family budget. There was a higher infant mortality rate in these regions and poorer hospital and education services. Most families lived in terrace houses with two rooms upstairs, two down, no bathroom and an outside lavatory often shared with other families. Dull food, poor clothing and grim surroundings made for a miserable life on the dole—yet even so it was better than life for the unemployed before the Great War.

LIFE FOR THE MORE PROSPEROUS

Although the South-east and Midlands enjoyed prosperity compared to the depressed regions, there were still many ordinary people living bleak lives. In 1936 one in three houses in Shoreditch had no indoor water supply and the state of evacuee children from London in 1939-40 showed how much poverty, dirt and disease still remained. Yet it was people in more prosperous areas who were more likely to be able to afford the better-quality council houses with their indoor bathrooms and lavatories. Here also lived many who were able to afford the private houses that made up three-quarters of house-building in the 1930's. Around many towns and cities the suburbs spread in long ribbon developments served by buses and cars. Many

THEY TRAVEL THE ROAD
(Jarrow unemployed march to London to petition the Government)
November 4th, 1936

Strube neatly shows that the eyes of those in power are firmly fixed on Europe, ignoring regional problems

new houses were three-bedroomed, semi-detached dwellings though there were larger properties, often built in a mock-Tudor style.

Electricity was increasingly used to light streets and houses, and to power railways. It made possible the purchase of labour-saving devices by the new householders—electric cookers and washing machines, vacuum cleaners and radios. Lower prices enabled people to eat better, and to consume more sugar, tea and meat, previously almost luxuries. More plentiful soap and soap powders improved the cleanliness of people and their clothes. Shoppers patronized large chain stores, bought more canned products and more cheap, mass-produced goods.

By 1939 about eleven million workers enjoyed holidays with pay. The mass entertainments of the 1920's expanded in the 1930's and to them were added Billy Butlin's 1937 scheme for holiday camps aimed especially at working people. Cinemas numbered 4,700 in 1937; newspapers fought for customers by offering free insurance, sets of Dickens' collected works, household goods or encyclopaedias; consumption of tobacco rose to 189 million lb in 1938 compared with 92 million lb in 1913. All these were signs of a changing way of life affecting most of the nation, not just the privileged few.

Newspapers and cinemas made more effort than the B.B.C. to win popular favour. It must have been a major struggle for newspaper owners to keep to themselves the 1936 crisis when the new king, Edward VIII, clashed with Baldwin over the King's determination to marry a twice-divorced American, Mrs Simpson. In December this issue at last became public news, and though Churchill, Beaver-

EDWARD'S FAREWELL

Below we reprint the historic farewell message which ex-King Edward broadcast from Windsor Castle on the night of Friday, December 11, 1936.

At long last I am able to say a few words of my own.

I have never wanted to withhold anything, but until now it has not been constitutionally possible for me to speak.

A few hours ago I discharged my last duty as King and Emperor, and now that I have been succeeded by my brother, the Duke of York, my first words must be to declare my allegiance to him.

This I do with all my heart.

You all know the reasons which have impelled me to renounce the Throne, but I want you to understand that in making up my mind I did not forget the country or the Empire, which as Prince of Wales and lately as King I have for twenty-five years tried to serve.

But you must believe me when I tell you that I have found it impossible to carry the heavy burden of responsibility and to discharge my duties as King as I would wish to do without the help and support of the woman I love.

And I want you to know that the decision I have made has been mine and mine alone. This was a thing I had to judge entirely for myself. The other person most nearly concerned has tried up to the last to persuade me to take a different course.

I have made this, the most serious decision of my life, only upon the single thought of what would in the end be best for all.

This decision has been made less difficult to me by the sure knowledge that my brother, with his long training in the public affairs of this country and with his fine qualities, will be able to take my place forthwith without interruption or injury to the life and progress of the Empire.

And he has one matchless blessing, enjoyed by so many of you and not bestowed on me—a happy home with his wife and children.

During these hard days I have been comforted by her Majesty, my mother, and by my family. The Ministers of the Crown, and in particular Mr. Baldwin, the Prime Minister, have always treated me with full consideration. There has never been any constitutional difference between me and them and between me and Parliament. Bred in the constitutional traditions by my father, I should never have allowed any such issue to arise.

Ever since I was Prince of Wales and later on when I occupied the Throne I have been treated with the greatest kindness by all classes of the people, wherever I have lived or journeyed throughout the Empire. For that I am very grateful.

I now quit altogether public affairs and I lay down my burden. It may be some time before I return to my native land, but I shall always follow the fortunes of the British race and Empire with profound interest, and if at any time in the future I can be found of service to his Majesty in a private station I shall not fail.

And now we all have a new king. I wish him and you, his people, happiness and prosperity with all my heart. God bless you all. GOD SAVE THE KING!

The Duke and Duchess of Windsor after their marriage

brook and others rallied to the King's cause, Baldwin successfully insisted that such a marriage was not acceptable. Edward was forced to abdicate and his place was taken by the frail, nervous and modest George VI.

Prosperous areas of Britain were attractive to new industries seeking to be near their markets and freed, by electricity, from the need to be near coalfields. Their employees were major producers and purchasers of that increasingly numerous product, the motor car. By 1934 there were so many cars that a Road Traffic Act introduced a driving test, insisted on certain safety features on cars (like windscreen wipers), and laid down the 30 m.p.h. maximum speed limit in built-up areas. The motor car represented one of the clearest signs of the decline of the old Britain. It demanded more roads, enabled towns and cities to sprawl and contributed to village decline by carrying people, in their leisure time, to towns for entertainment. As the author J. B. Priestley remarked, these prosperous car-using Britons were a new social group whose style of life was different from that of many of the rural and industrial communities.

Cheaper cars meant busy roads, and soon many major and minor road works had to be undertaken

Documentary Six

A middle-class Liverpool family face hard times

The home is still middle-class, as is the appearance and clothing of the household: but the furniture has gradually gone, an £85 piano fetching £35, a £30 bedroom suite £9, an £18 sewing machine £3. There is nearly £4 owing on the rent; there are debts for groceries—although relations help. All insurances have been realized . . . He conceals the fact of his having been out of work from all his friends, if possible, and from his neighbours, and even the boy is not allowed to know the real position.

From MEN WITHOUT WORK 1938, by the Pilgrim Trust
Reprinted by permission of Cambridge University Press

An out-of-work Welsh collier

A collier, aged 37, who served 3 years in the war and has done no work whatever for five years. He is described as wiry and very fit . . . But unemployed men are not simply units of employability who can, through the medium of the dole, be put into cold storage and taken out again immediately they are needed. While they are in cold storage, things are liable to happen to them. In the case of this man what has happened was that the 'will to work' had been affected.

From MEN WITHOUT WORK 1938, by the Pilgrim Trust

The 'new' England

The third England, I concluded, was the new post-war England, belonging far more to the age itself than to this particular island. America, I suppose, was its real birth-place. This is the England of arterial and by-pass roads, of filling stations and factories that look like exhibition buildings, of giant cinemas and dance halls and cafes, bungalows with tiny garages, cocktail bars, Woolworths, motor coaches, wireless, hiking, factory girls looking like actresses, greyhound racing and dirt tracks, swimming pools, and everything given away for cigarette coupons.

From ENGLISH JOURNEY by J. B. Priestley, 1934
Reprinted by permission of William Heinemann Ltd.

Social change in Britain in the 1930's

Few people in modern England own anything at all except clothes, furniture, and possibly a house. The peasantry have long since disappeared, the independent shopkeeper is being destroyed, the small businessman is diminishing in numbers. But at the same time modern industry is so complicated that it cannot get along without great numbers of managers, salesmen, engineers, chemists and technicians of all kinds, drawing fairly large salaries. . . . To an increasing extent the rich and the poor read the same books, and they also see the same films and listen to the same radio programmes. And the differences in their way of life have been diminished by the mass production of cheap clothes and improvements in housing . . .

After 1918 there began to appear something that had never existed in England before: people of indeterminate social class. In 1910 every human being in these islands could be 'placed' in an instant by his clothes, manners and accent. That is no longer the case.

From THE LION AND THE UNICORN by George Orwell, 1941
Reprinted by permission of Secker and Warburg Ltd. and
Mrs Sonia Brownell Orwell

GENERAL PROBLEMS OF FOREIGN POLICY

Though victorious in the Great War and with an Empire bigger than ever before, Britain was to find post-war foreign and imperial difficulties just as awkward to solve as domestic social and economic problems. Britain's armed forces were reduced very rapidly once the war ended in 1918 and thereafter left in poor shape until 1934. Britain was, therefore, in no fit state to fight any kind of major war for much of the inter-war period. The memory of the horrors of the Great War together with fear of what air attacks might do in any new European war made Britain shrink from acting aggressively.

" YOU'VE GOT TO ADMIT I'M BRINGING PEACE TO THE POOR SUFFERING BASQUES."

The destruction of Guernica in 1937 caused an outcry throughout the world

Instead all British governments in the period 1918-39 tried to solve problems abroad by what came to be known much later as 'appeasement'. For most of this period such a policy did not mean cringing before a bullying rival but rather seeking, by peaceful discussion, to put right reasonable grievances felt by other countries. Appeasement was to British governments, therefore, both morally right and economically sensible.

Powerful rivals threatened Britain's position as a world power. By 1918 the military strength of the U.S.A. and of Japan was impressive; from 1922 (when Mussolini gained power) Italy seemed increasingly formidable. In Europe a huge French army remained in arms and from the early 1930's highly effective German forces were built up. In Europe, in the Mediterranean and in the Far East, then, there were possible rivals and Britain could not be militarily strong in all these areas at once. Yet Britain lacked adequate allies to make up for her own weakness. She shrank from tying herself to France, disliking French determination to keep Germany weak in Europe. Many in Britain soon came to see France as the threat to peace in Europe, not Germany or Italy. There was little understanding in Britain of French struggles to find security. The United States refused to commit herself to European alliances, yet partly because of U.S. pressure Britain had offended Japan by failing to renew her alliance with her.

This left Britain dependent on her Empire. Many imperial lands had helped Britain in the Great War, but once war was over they disarmed rapidly. Australia and New Zealand looked to Britain for protection; South Africa and Canada felt it unlikely they would need British help: all four made it clear they would not automatically come to Britain's aid in the future. By the 1931 Statute of Westminster the independence of these dominions was officially recognized (they were merely bound by recognizing the same monarch) but they had been acting quite independently since 1918. The rest of Britain's Empire ate up British strength rather than added to it. In India and the Middle East especially, Britain had to station much of her army to control nationalist movements.

Inter-war British governments led a country repelled by the thought of war, weakened by economic troubles in a world where dangerous rivals were increasingly active.

IMPERIAL APPEASEMENT

British governments preferred to try to hold the dominions together in an appearance of unity rather than face the fact that Canada and South Africa in particular saw little need for British ties. Australia and New Zealand were more aware of their weakness and it was partly to please them that the costly military base of Singapore was developed. Dominion pressure was repeatedly put on Britain to try to keep her from becoming entangled in Continental affairs and British ministers usually took serious notice of this pressure.

In the Middle East and India the British developed a policy of appeasement to try to solve the problem of growing nationalist movements. Indian nationalism had once been a largely middle-class affair led by the Congress Party; after 1918 under the leadership of Gandhi it became a much more popular mass movement. Though Gandhi was a highly intelligent and well-educated lawyer, he dressed and lived very simply and managed to win the support of many Indian peasants. His methods of using peaceful demonstrations and peaceful refusals to co-operate with British rule, proved very difficult to deal with. Though Gandhi and many of his followers were put in prison, the British shrank from being really ruthless. Instead both Labour and Baldwin's Conservatives agreed on negotiations by the Viceroy, Lord Irwin, with Indian leaders. From these discussions the 1935 Government of India Act emerged giving almost full control of local government to Indians themselves. Central government remained in the Viceroy's hands, Congress continued to demand more power; the British government responded with vague promises that India would eventually develop to reach full dominion status. These changes were too much for the right wing of the Conservative Party and they followed Winston Churchill's lead in protesting vigorously but in vain; Churchill's quarrels over India, like his differences over the question of Edward VIII's abdication, helped keep him out of office.

In Egypt Britain was also ready to give way to pressure, but not to give way sufficiently to satisfy Egyptian nationalists. In particular Egyptians objected to Britain's policy of developing the Sudan as a separate region free from Egyptian influence. In nearby Palestine even more serious developments were taking place. As a British mandate, Palestine had become the home of increasing numbers of

Jewish immigrants, to the great alarm of local Arab peoples. A suggestion in 1930, by a Labour minister, Lord Passfield, that immigration should stop, failed—indeed the number of immigrants increased as Nazi persecution of Jews drove many to leave Germany. A 1937 Royal Commission suggested a division of Palestine; a later commission decided this was not practicable. In 1939 the British government decided it needed the support of the Arabs and attempted to appease them by promising an end to Jewish immigration once another 75,000 had come to Palestine. Britain had to station many of her forces abroad because of her Empire, where they became tied up in regions many thousands of miles from Western Europe. All this increased British reluctance to act vigorously in Europe; the strength to do so was simply not there.

A PERIOD OF SUCCESS?

Until 1931 British policy seemed to work reasonably well. Most people soon agreed that the Treaties of Paris had been too harsh and that Germany should be allowed to develop as an equal and reasonably flourishing neighbour. Austen Chamberlain (Foreign Secretary from 1924) continued Ramsay MacDonald's policy of building good relations with both France and Germany. In October 1925 Britain signed the Locarno Treaty by which she and Italy guaranteed the frontiers between Germany, Belgium and France. In 1928 many countries signed the Kellogg-Briand Pact which rejected the use of force as a means of solving problems. In 1930 the army of occupation left Germany's Rhineland and the Young Plan cut German reparations by about 20 per cent to £100 million a year to be paid for 59 years. Whilst Arthur Henderson worked on this success, MacDonald visited the U.S.A. and signed a new naval agreement.

MacDonald, Chamberlain and Henderson all seemed to care about the League of Nations and to have achieved much, yet behind all they had done there lay massive unsolved problems. Not only did Locarno do nothing about settling Germany's eastern frontier (yet this was the frontier she most resented), it contained no real way of working effectively should it be violated. British ministers entered into agreements which their country lacked the means of enforcing. Disarmament conferences that met for much of this period made no real progress, though countries were ready to sign a document as vague as the Kellogg-Briand Pact. This period of peace was shattered by the Great Depression: it depended heavily on goodwill between German and French governments and after 1929 this soon vanished.

THE DIFFICULTIES OF THE THIRTIES

As world economic troubles worsened after 1929, so there were changes in several countries that made more extreme—even violent—action acceptable in foreign affairs. Japan's government came increasingly under the army's influence and the army saw conquests in China as the way to find space for Japanese people to colonize, and to provide economic resources for Japanese industry. This affected British interests in China and South-East Asia, yet Britain had not the power to halt Japan, nor would the United States do anything positive.

In Europe there were changes too. Mussolini's rule in Italy had not alarmed British governments—indeed many commentators approved of his attacks on corruption in Italian affairs and the success he seemed to have had in improving Italy's economy and armed forces. That the two countries should remain friendly seemed vital, for the Mediterranean was not only a source of trade, it was the route to the Middle East and India. But the depression helped wreck parliamentary government in Germany by increasing unemployment, ruining many of the middle-class and making many Germans ready to vote for extremists such as Nazis or Communists. Out of a struggle for power there emerged, in January 1933, a successful Nazi Party led by the new Chancellor of Germany, Adolf Hitler. By August 1934 Hitler had made himself Germany's Fuhrer —her leader of government and armed forces. His policies were aimed at rebuilding German self-confidence and national pride by undoing much of the Treaty of Versailles, rearming and leaving the League (which it was allowed to join in 1926), and persecuting Jews in Germany as scapegoats to be blamed for nearly all the country's troubles.

Though well informed by their ambassador about Hitler's personality and the Nazi Party's aims, the leaders of the British government were apparently not alarmed by events in Germany. They disliked Communism even more than Fascism and Hitler promised to make

President von Hindenburg receives Hitler as Chancellor, January 1933

Germany a mighty obstacle to Communism's westward spread. His wild speeches and violent demands could be explained as expressions on behalf of a people angry at the unjust treatment of the Versailles Treaty. British politicians felt nervous enough to begin planning a small rearmament programme in 1934, but basically they hoped that Hitler would calm down if Germany's reasonable grievances were satisfied.

THE MANCHURIAN CRISIS

In September 1931, Japan—a key member of the League of Nations —opened a campaign against another League member in the province of Manchuria. China was an ill-governed republic in which Britain herself had used force and Britain was slow to condemn

Japan. When it gradually became clear that Japan was bent on conquest, not just the protection of her interests, then Britain supported the League's Lytton Commission in condemning Japan. The event showed how feeble both the League and Britain herself were: the U.S.A. refused to act, and nothing could be done to stop the Japanese.

The early 1930's was a time of powerful anti-war movements in Britain. Labour was led by a pacifist, George Lansbury, and at East Fulham in October 1933 there was a by-election that many believed proved popular dislike of war. In the same year the Oxford Union voted 'This House will not fight for King and Country' and in the following year a League of Nations poll—the 'Peace Ballot'— showed large support for the League and great division about whether force should be used to tackle an aggressor.

When government spending on rearmament began to go up in 1934, the result was widespread criticism of the ministry. There was, then, never any question of taking any action against Japan. The Japanese were able to turn Manchuria into a puppet state and, in 1936, to launch wider attacks. The feeble grumbles of Britain and France irritated the Japanese and encouraged them to become more friendly with Germany instead.

ABYSSINIA AND THE RHINELAND

In 1935 Mussolini demonstrated the power of his state by attacking Abyssinia. Abyssinia was a backward land whose entry to the League Britain had not welcomed, and the British themselves controlled massive African conquests. But the mood in inter-war Britain was very much against actions like those of Mussolini. The Foreign Secretary, Sir Samuel Hoare, found it very difficult to respond to this mood and yet keep Italian friendship. In a general election in autumn 1935, the coalition promised strong support for the League and won the election easily.

Yet speeches did not stop Mussolini, nor did banning trade with Italy in certain items. Vital oil supplies on which Italian forces depended were not stopped for fear that the Italians would attack British Mediterranean interests. Hoare, like Laval his French counterpart, tried to resolve the situation. Between them they drew up a plan to try to halt Mussolini by offering him half of Abyssinia

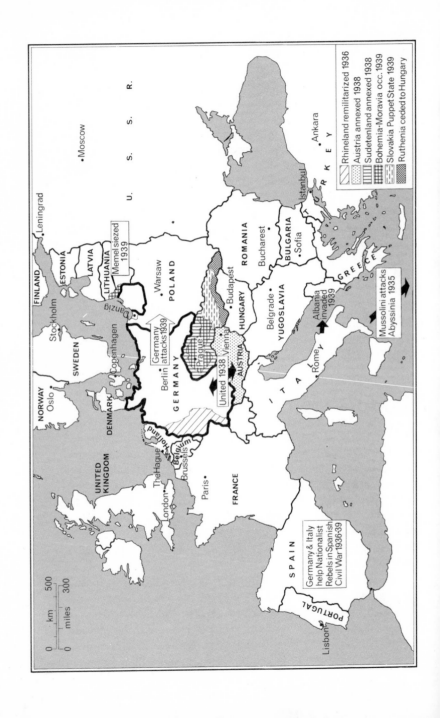

and economic control of the rest. Yet the news of this raised such widespread anger in Britain and France that Hoare's colleagues hastily rejected the plan and Hoare was forced to resign. His place was taken by the 37-year-old Minister for League affairs, Anthony Eden.

Britain's reputation suffered severely in this episode. Mussolini went on to conquer the whole of Abyssinia, feeling irritation with Britain for protesting and applying some trade sanctions, and contempt that Britain seemed, in the end, to be so feeble. The friendship of Italy and Britain had been shown in 1935 when the two countries, together with France, had joined to denounce Hitler's attacks on the Treaty of Versailles and his declaration that Germany would rearm and would swell her forces by using conscripts. The

Benito Mussolini

Abyssinian affair drove Mussolini closer to Hitler for Hitler did not attack his policy. In any case the selfishness of British policy seemed clear because five months after the Stresa agreement objecting to German rearmament, Britain accepted German naval rebuilding (including 20 submarines) provided it did not total more than 35 per cent of the tonnage of Britain's fleets.

Whilst Abyssinia dominated affairs, Hitler struck another blow at the Versailles Treaty. In March 1936 his army chiefs' fears were swept aside and German troops moved into the Rhineland. Despite the fact that it was supposed to be a demilitarized area, British leaders found it impossible to see anything dreadful in German troops reoccupying part of their own country. The French were more alarmed, but the slump had upset French affairs too and left them far less ready to act than they had been in the 1920's. Though their army was far bigger than Hitler's, the French stood by and watched as German troops moved right up to the Rhine.

THE SPANISH CIVIL WAR

Events in Spain drew Germany and Italy more closely together. In July 1936 units of the Spanish Army led by General Franco's Army of Morocco rose in rebellion against the Spanish government. The rebels received support from many Church leaders, the Spanish Fascist Party and most of Spain's well-to-do. Against the rebels were ranged an alliance of republicans, socialists, anarchists and communists.

Eden's policy towards Spain reflected British determination to keep out of trouble, for he took the lead in setting up in London a Non-Intervention Committee to leave Spain to settle her own affairs. Britain never had any intention of acting directly in Spain and could not even make non-intervention work. To Hitler and Mussolini the Spanish Civil War offered a chance to try out their armed forces and establish on France's south-west frontier a country friendly to themselves. Thousands of Italian troops went to Spain and Spanish forces were equipped by Italian supplies. Hitler provided war supplies and expert help too; in particular he sent the Condor Legion to equip Franco with air power. In reply the Russians began to send aid to the Spanish government, yet they, like Italy and Germany, were members of the Non-Intervention Committee.

Non-intervention became a farce with naval patrols that could easily be dodged and the sinking of vessels trading with Spanish government ports by mysterious submarines. These sinkings in fact drove Britain, France and the U.S.S.R. to sign the Nyon Agreement for firmer action in the Western Mediterranean and their patrols put a stop to the destruction of neutral vessels. So fearful was Britain that the Spanish Civil War might spread to involve others that she persuaded France's Socialist government to close her frontiers to the supply of arms to Spain's government.

Yet the war did affect Britain. Thousands of volunteers poured into Spain to help the government by forming International Brigades and 2,000 of these volunteers were British. Half of these volunteers were Communists: 500 of them died, including the poet John Cornford; even more were injured, among them the writer George Orwell. The war split Britain between those who saw it as a struggle to keep back Communism and anarchy and those who saw it as a battle against the fascist menace. British government sympathies tended to be with the rebels, but left-wing support for the Spanish government continued the conversion from pacifism that the Abyssinian affair had begun. In 1935 George Lansbury, the Labour leader of the time, was forced out of the leadership and replaced by Clement Attlee.

The civil war dragged on until Franco's final victory in 1939. British behaviour encouraged Hitler and Mussolini to regard Britain with contempt and wrecked British efforts to recover Mussolini's goodwill.

By the mid 1930's British foreign policy was floundering. Disarmament conferences were finished and the League shown to be unable to deal with powerful aggressors. Three powerful rivals had appeared and in the Far East, the Mediterranean and on the Continent British interests were threatened. Yet Britain doubted her ability to face even one of these, let alone all three.

By 1934 Stanley Baldwin had come to believe that Britain must rearm. Yet he was too sensitive to popular feelings to push his beliefs vigorously. Few in his party had any time for Churchill's cries of alarm and demands for a much bigger arms programme. Labour continued to attack rearmament, the Treasury complained of its cost and as a result progress was very slow. In 1936 Fighter Command was established under Dowding, but Baldwin put little faith in the ability of fighters to stop bombers. A programme of building big four-engined bombers was drawn up which, it was hoped, would deter aggressors from striking at Britain. Expanding both army and navy involved increasing their size, providing new weapons, and completing the Singapore base. Yet when Baldwin resigned in May 1937, weary from many years of political struggle, Britain was far from ready for war. Her industries were not geared to war production and were unable to provide many essential items. Her forces had become so run down that out-of-date bi-planes and an army equipped with few tanks faced heavy odds. Some blame for this may well have been Baldwin's, yet most of the nation still seemed to shrink from facing the cost of rearmament and the harsh realities of Britain's weakness in world affairs.

Documentary Seven

Churchill's views on Indian reforms given in the House of Commons on 26th January 1931

After all, there are British rights and interests in India. Two centuries of effort and achievement, lives given on a hundred fields, far more lives given and consumed in faithful and devoted service to the Indian people themselves. All this has earned us rights of our own in India. . . . When the nation sees our individual fellow countrymen scattered about, with their women and children . . . in hourly peril amidst the Indian multitudes, when, at any moment, this may produce shocking scenes, then I think there will be a sharp awakening. That, Sir, is an ending which I trust and pray we may avoid, but it is an ending to which step by step and day by day, we are remorselessly and fatuously conducted.

Part of the Statute of Westminster, 1931

The Crown is the symbol of the free association of the members of the British Commonwealth . . . they are united by a common allegiance to the Crown . . . no law hereafter made by the Parliament of the United Kingdom shall extend to any of the said Dominions as part of the law of that Dominion otherwise than at the request and with the consent of that Dominion . . .

The expression 'Dominion' means any of the following Dominions, that is to say, the Dominion of Canada, the Commonwealth of Australia, the Dominion of New Zealand, the Union of South Africa, the Irish Free State and Newfoundland.

Reprinted by permission of HMSO

Baldwin drops the Hoare-Laval Pact: an extract from his speech in the House of Commons on 18th December 1935

There could not be the support in this country behind those proposals even as terms of negotiation. I felt that there could not be that volume of popular opinion which it is necessary to have in a democracy behind the Government in a matter so important as this. It is perfectly obvious now that the proposals are absolutely and completely dead.

The problem of the Far East

The very people like Bob Cecil who have made us disarm, and quite right too, are urging us forward to take action. But where will action lead us to? If you enforce an economic boycott you will have war declared by Japan and she will seize Singapore and Hong Kong and we cannot, as we are placed, stop her. You will get nothing out of Washington but words, big words, but only words.

> Stanley Baldwin 27 February 1932 speaking to Tom Jones
> From DIARY WITH LETTERS by Tom Jones
> Reprinted by permission of Oxford University Press

Sir Austen Chamberlain attacks Nazism: an extract from a speech in the House of Commons on 13th April 1933

What is this new spirit of German nationalism? The worst of the all-Prussian Imperialism, with an added savagery, a racial pride, an exclusiveness which cannot allow any fellow-subject not of 'pure Nordic birth' equality of rights and citizenship within the nation to which he belongs. Are you going to discuss revision with a government like that? Germany is afflicted by this narrow, exclusive, aggressive spirit, by which it is a crime to be in favour of peace and a crime to be a Jew. This is not a Germany to which one can afford to make concessions.

Eden's impression of Hitler in 1934

Smaller and slighter than I had expected from his photographs, his appearance was smart, almost dapper, despite his incongruous uniform. Hitler impressed me during these discussions as much more than a demagogue. He knew what he was speaking about . . . Hitler declared that Germany had no interest in aggression. The war had taught his country that it was easier to destroy than to build up, and this formerly militarist people now saw that peace ought to be the permanent state of mankind. For all I then knew these sentiments might be sincere.

> From FACING THE DICTATORS by Anthony Eden
> Reprinted by permission of Cassell & Co. Ltd.

The military problem facing Britain

We are in a position of having threats at both ends of the Empire from strong military powers i.e. Germany and Japan, while in the centre we have lost our traditional security in the Mediterranean . . . So long as that position remains unresolved diplomatically, only very great military and financial strength can give the Empire security.

Annual review of the Chiefs of Staff 1937
Reprinted by permission of HMSO

British support to the League of Nations

In 1934 Cecil had organised the 'Nationa' Declaration on the League of Nations and Armaments', popularly called 'The Peace Ballot'. The League of Nations Union, with the help of many national organisations, including the Labour and Liberal parties and some leading Conservatives, invited every British citizen over 18 to give answers to six questions concerning British membership of the League, international disarmament, economic and military sanctions against aggression.

Journalists thought it unlikely to succeed, and that the target of five million votes was wildly optimistic. In fact, more than eleven and half million votes were recorded.

The answers were over 90% in favour of the League, disarmament and the abolition of private manufacture of arms; over 80% for the abolition of air forces; over 90% for economic sanctions, and 74% for military sanctions, against aggression. The vote was recognised by everyone to be of great significance, and it produced a profound effect upon the Baldwin government.

From Philip Noel-Baker's article in
THE BALDWIN AGE edited by John Raymond
Reprinted by permission of Eyre & Spottiswoode

The National Government's Election Manifesto of 1935:
extracts relating to The League

*The League of Nations will remain . . . the keystone of British foreign
policy. . . . Our attitude to the League is dictated by the conviction that
collective security by collective action can alone save us from a return
to the old system which resulted in the Great War. . . .*

*We shall continue to do all in our power to uphold the Covenant and
to maintain and increase the efficiency of the League. In the present
unhappy dispute between Italy and Abyssinia, there will be no waver-
ing in the policy we have hitherto pursued. We shall take no action in
isolation, but we shall be prepared faithfully to take our part in any
collective action decided upon by the League and shared by its members.*

Clement Attlee's comment—from a speech on 28th June 1936

*The Government has decided to lead in the surrender to force. This has
killed the collective system. While they refuse to say what their future
policy is to be, it is clear from Mr Chamberlain's speech that they aim
at reforming the League so as to make it safe for aggression.*

Winston Churchill—in the House of Commons on 5th October
1938

*When I think of the fair hopes of a long peace which still lay before
Europe at the beginning of 1933 when Herr Hitler first obtained power,
and of all the opportunities of arresting the growth of Nazi power which
have been thrown away . . . I cannot believe that a parallel exists in the
whole course of history. So far as this country is concerned, the responsibility must rest with those who have had the undisputed control of our
political affairs . . . They exploited and discredited the vast institution
of the League of Nations and they neglected to make alliances and
combinations which might have repaired previous errors, and thus they
left us in the hour of trial without adequate national defence or effective
international security.*

NEVILLE CHAMBERLAIN

In May 1937, Neville Chamberlain became Prime Minister and at once set about changing Britain's foreign policy. Unlike Baldwin, Chamberlain could not bear to let British policy drift and could not tolerate men in the government with whom he seriously disagreed. He was a very hard-working Prime Minister whose colleagues respected his skill and ability, but he was not generally very popular. Chamberlain was a shy and solitary man, he spent little time winning the friendship of ordinary M.P.s and even less time on winning the support of the public at large.

Chamberlain developed his foreign policy with the help of a small group of colleagues, and these colleagues tended to be men who did not really question what their leader did. They included the Chancellor of the Exchequer, Sir John Simon, the Home Secretary, Sir Samuel Hoare, and a new Foreign Secretary, Lord Halifax. Anthony Eden, who had been Foreign Secretary when Chamberlain became Prime Minister, resigned because he disliked the way the running of affairs was increasingly taken from him, and especially the vigorous way Chamberlain tried to win the friendship of Mussolini. The Prime Minister also put much trust in Sir Horace Wilson, the government's Chief Industrial Adviser, and Nevile Henderson, the British Ambassador in Germany. Wilson agreed fully with his leader's policies whilst Henderson was very impressed with German strength and seemed eager to please Germany's Nazi leaders.

Chamberlain had played a big part in developing the rearmament programme in Britain; yet he still felt his country to be very weak. He was aware that the Dominions were very reluctant to be dragged into Britain's affairs in Europe, and he hated the cost of the arms programme. No one could doubt that the Prime Minister cared deeply about peace for, like many other M.P.s, he had strong memories of the Great War. Above all, Chamberlain was a practical man. The League of Nations seemed to him to be of little value, and dealing directly with Italy and Germany in order to settle their complaints peacefully seemed to him to be the sensible course to follow.

REARMAMENT AND THE OPPONENTS OF APPEASEMENT

Chamberlain altered the arms programme to put much more emphasis on the defence of Britain. Most money went into building fighters for the R.A.F. and as a result the building of bombers was held up. Though this led to the production of Spitfires and Hurricanes, it was not until 1939 that they appeared in any numbers, for British industry was not yet ready to manufacture many aircraft. Chamberlain feared the bombing of Britain more than any other aspect of modern war. He over-rated the German Luftwaffe's power and thought 60 days' bombing of Britain would kill and injure 1,800,000 civilians. (In fact in the whole Second World War British civilians killed and wounded numbered under 300,000.) Chamberlain doubted whether even the stronger fighter and radar defences would stop German bombers.

Spending money on the R.A.F. meant that the army was neglected and British defences in the Far East largely ignored. Faced with a possible war in which Germany, Italy and Japan might all be enemies, Chamberlain felt Britain had to concentrate first on her own defence and then on the defence of the Empire. The result was that as the Prime Minister tried to do more to solve the problems in Europe, Britain had no army that might worry European countries, whilst her bomber force was feeble and out of date.

To those who criticized him, Chamberlain put the question, what else could be done? Upon whom could Britain rely? The Dominions spent little on arms and did not seem to want to be involved in Europe. President Roosevelt of the U.S.A. suggested a world conference to discuss grievances but Chamberlain snubbed him, and indeed there was no sign at all that the U.S.A. was prepared to do anything effective. Many people in Britain—and especially in the Conservative Party—disliked Stalin's Russia, whilst a close alliance with France had been something that most British politicians had avoided since 1918. Few Conservatives joined Winston Churchill in his criticisms of the government, and even Churchill was often vague about how Britain was actually going to do anything effective. The Labour Party was only just beginning to stop criticizing the whole rearmament programme and was finding it difficult to agree on a new line of foreign policy. Chamberlain, therefore, had much freedom in which to follow his policy of seeking to solve problems before they became too serious.

THE AUSTRIAN CRISIS

As German strength grew, so Hitler became more confident in seizing chances to extend Germany's frontiers. By 1938 he had become sufficiently friendly with Mussolini to feel that Italy would not try to stop a German bid to gain control of Austria. He bullied the Austrian Chancellor, Schuschnigg, into taking Seyss Inquart, leader of Austria's Nazis, into his government. When Schuschnigg planned to ask for a vote of the whole Austrian people, Hitler threatened to use force against him: the Chancellor resigned. Seyss Inquart took his place, promptly invited German troops into his country and Hitler was able, in March 1938, to unite Austria to Germany, despite the fact that the Treaty of Versailles forbade this.

Chamberlain never seriously considered resisting Hitler over the Austrian question. Yet taking Austria made it easier for Hitler to bully Czechoslovakia and also prevented Chamberlain from winning Italy's friendship by arguing that the two countries must stand together to keep Austria from German control and thus keep German troops from moving right up to Italy's frontiers. The Austrian success encouraged Hitler to feel he could attack new targets and depressed the Russian Foreign Minister, Litvinov, whose pleas for a conference of Russia, Britain and France to plan how to resist further Nazi aggression were ignored by Chamberlain.

THE CZECHOSLOVAKIA QUESTION

Czechoslovakia had been created after the Great War from part of the old Austrian Empire. Its population included not only Czechs, but also Slovaks, Magyars, Ruthenes, Poles, and $3\frac{1}{2}$ million Germans. The bulk of these Germans lived in the Sudetenland, a strip of

Czechoslovakia awaits invasion

western Czechoslovakia that contained vital mountain defences and much of the country's industry. In this region, a Nazi party led by Konrad Henlein had grown up and was, by 1938, declaring that Germans in Czechoslovakia were being ill-treated and should be given all sorts of privileges.

Czechoslovakia's defence lay in the hands of a modern army of 35 divisions, equipped by the excellent Skoda arms works. In addition, her democratic government, led by Benes, expected help from two allies, France and Russia. But to Chamberlain, the Czech question seemed a dangerous flashpoint where a war might break out into which Britain might be dragged. The French government, headed by Daladier and represented in foreign affairs by Bonnet, felt itself too weak to resist Germany without British help and let Chamberlain lead the way in policy making. For Czechoslovakia, the Prime Minister cared little; nor did he try to win over Russia, yet Russia was the country best placed to help the Czechs. He devoted his energies to pressing the Czechs to give way peacefully, yet when they offered Henlein internal self-government for the Sudetenland, Hitler merely raised his demands and stirred up a rising in the Sudetenland. The rising was easily dealt with and Henlein fled to Germany, but Hitler now wanted vengeance against the Czech government.

THE MUNICH CRISIS

In an attempt to persuade Hitler to accept a peaceful settlement, the 69-year-old Chamberlain set off on his first aircraft flight and met Hitler in Germany on 15th September 1938. Hitler's terms seemed to him to be reasonable; he returned to persuade his Cabinet and the French to accept them, and then returned to Germany. But by now Hitler had raised his demands, declaring that German troops should go into the Sudetenland in the very near future and that the Czechs would obtain no compensation. This was too much for Chamberlain; he returned gloomily home whilst the Czech army prepared to fight, war preparations went ahead in France, and in Britain gas masks and helmets were distributed and anti-aircraft defences improved.

The Prime Minister clearly felt horrified that war seemed likely over an issue he described as 'a quarrel in a far away country between people of whom we know nothing'. He made new efforts to call for meetings and was rewarded on 28th September when, whilst addressing the House of Commons, he received a message that Hitler had agreed to a conference at Munich with British, French and Italian representatives.

On 29th September the leaders of these four countries met to settle Czechoslovakia's future. The Czechs themselves were not consulted and waited to hear their fate. The final agreement gave Hitler all he wanted without striking a blow, and drove the Czech leader Benes to resign. Allowing the Sudetenland to be taken by Germany meant that the rest of Czechoslovakia was defenceless, yet Britain and France now joined in giving guarantees to Czechoslovakia. Such guarantees depended simply on German goodwill, and Hitler was ready enough with empty promises. His generals felt relieved that war had been avoided, for they knew the limited state of German war-preparedness, and the weakness of Germany's defences in the west.

Many of the population and most M.P.s cheered Chamberlain's return and, carried away by such popularity, he spoke of having won 'peace with honour' and 'peace in our time'. Only Duff Cooper resigned from the government, a mere 30 Conservatives abstained from voting on the Munich question, and congratulations poured in from the King, the Pope, the Dominions and the U.S.A. Finally, Chamberlain was able to produce a piece of paper signed by Hitler

We, the German Führer and Chancellor and the
British Prime Minister, have had a further
meeting today and are agreed in recognising that
the question of Anglo-German relations is of the
first importance for the two countries and for
Europe.

We regard the agreement signed last night
and the Anglo-German Naval Agreement as symbolic
of the desire of our two peoples never to go to
war with one another again.

We are resolved that the method of
consultation shall be the method adopted to deal
with any other questions that may concern our two
countries, and we are determined to continue our
efforts to remove possible sources of difference
and thus to contribute to assure the peace of
Europe.

September 30, 1938.

The Munich agreement

in which he promised that Britain and Germany would never go to
war again.

THE END OF APPEASEMENT

Avoiding war meant that British air, radar and anti-aircraft defences
could be improved, yet it gave more time to Germany too, and
greatly encouraged Britain's enemies. Hitler now believed he could
do much as he liked in Eastern Europe as long as Chamberlain was
in charge of British affairs, and he also sent more help to Franco in
Spain. In the Far East, Japan launched new attacks on China about
which Britain could do nothing and Hitler's confidence was shown

in early 1939 when German forces took over the bulk of the rest of Czechoslovakia, allowing small areas of land to go to Poland and Hungary too.

By this act, however, Hitler had shown the emptiness of his promises to Britain. The land he now took was not largely German inhabited and could in no way be called rightfully German. Lord Halifax expressed dismay, Liberal and Labour men argued that justice now clearly lay with the Czechs and the mood in the Conservative party and in the whole country began to change. Chamberlain himself still favoured peaceful negotiations and hoped to calm down Hitler by handing back part of Germany's former African empire. But there were now many pressures on him at home urging him to drop appeasement; for he was no longer free to negotiate as he pleased, nor could Britain escape, by 1939, the mounting evidence of German brutality to Jews.

In March 1939 Hitler turned on Lithuania and bullied her into handing back Memel to Germany. In April, Mussolini despatched the Italian army to take over Albania. All hope that the greed of these two men would ever be satisfied seemed empty.

THE POLISH QUESTION

German pressure was now directed against Poland in order to recover the German-inhabited free city of Danzig together with land that would link Danzig to the rest of Germany. Whereas Czechoslovakia had been a parliamentary democracy with a modern army, Poland was a dictatorship whose army was woefully out of date, yet it was to this country that Britain and France, on 31st March 1939, gave the guarantees they had denied Czechoslovakia.

By giving guarantees, Chamberlain hoped both to deter Hitler and be able to settle peacefully a cause in which he thought much justice lay with Germany. But Beck, Poland's Foreign Minister, refused to offer anything Hitler was likely to accept and Hitler was unable to believe that Britain and France would really go to war to help Poland. In April and May, guarantees were given to Greece, Rumania and Turkey too, adding up to a formidable list of commitments for a country with as small an army as Britain. Sir John Simon, the Chancellor, gave the Cabinet lectures on Britain's economic weakness and the military leaders warned that Britain could not face Italy and Germany at once. Nor was any effort made to hold serious military talks with the Poles; Chamberlain was trying to bluff Hitler and Hitler was not to be deceived.

The one country that could help Poland was Russia, yet though Britain at last began talks with Russia, they were conducted in so leisurely a fashion that it was hard for Russia to take them seriously. The replacement (in charge of Russian affairs) of the pro-Western Litvinov by Molotov showed that Russia was despairing of ever uniting with the West against the Fascist countries. British leaders were still very suspicious of Communist Russia and thought little of the Russian Army since Stalin had executed most of its senior officers. In retrospect it was perhaps not surprising that the Russians sought safety in a deal with Germany on 27th August in which each agreed to remain neutral if the other went to war. Stalin and Hitler had been bitter opponents but now Stalin was promised part of Poland, whilst Hitler had a free hand to over-run the rest of that country.

THE COMING OF WAR

In vain Chamberlain and Daladier, Premier of France, tried to press for negotiations between Hitler and the Polish government. Hitler felt confident about solving the matter by force and, on 1st September 1939, after carefully staged incidents by Germans that would create an excuse for attack, German troops moved over the border and bombers attacked Warsaw. The crisis forced Chamberlain to reorganize his government to bring in some of his critics including Churchill (as First Lord of the Admiralty) and Eden (as Dominions Secretary). He could not persuade Hitler to withdraw and negotiate and thus was forced to declare war on 3rd September.

France declared war soon after Britain, yet neither country did anything to help the Poles as German forces rapidly gained the upper hand over them. A mere four divisions of British troops could be sent to help the French and the French themselves stayed behind their Maginot Line defences. Ageing British bombers flew over Germany—but only to drop leaflets. Chamberlain increased government control, introduced conscription, and put Sir John Anderson in charge of air raid defences; but he could not bring any drive or energy to running the war, he shrank from ruthless action and was incapable of inspiring popularity.

Chamberlain announces that Britain has declared war on Germany

In April 1940, with the war in the east won, German forces seized Denmark and Norway. Britain's attempts to block the Germans in Norway showed up all the defects of British planning and equipment and met with no success other than the destruction of a number of German ships. On 10th May German forces attacked Holland and Belgium and Chamberlain resigned. Once the war began he had been increasingly tired and depressed and under growing attack from Conservatives, as well as Labour and Liberal M.P.s. The other parties would not serve under Chamberlain as members of a coalition and the man who emerged to lead the new coalition government was Winston Churchill.

Though it is easy to criticize Chamberlain for being too vain and secretive, for giving in too easily to Hitler and over-rating his opponents too readily, it is hard to suggest what else he might have done but negotiate. Even had he urged war over the Czech issue, Britain had not the means to help the Czechs and the French had no plans for this kind of situation. Chamberlain had to face the problems of unemployment and depression at home, an Empire that seemed weak and difficult to protect, and the direct threat to Britain of air power. In the last resort, Britain simply did not have the means to live up to the world and European rôle she tried to play in the inter-war years.

Documentary Eight

Neville Chamberlain

His voice has a quality of harshness and with an occasional rasp, and is without music or seductive charm. His speech is lucid, competent, cogent, never rising to oratory, unadorned with fancy and rarely touched with emotion. But it gives a sense of mastery of what it attempts, well reflects the orderly mind behind.

A. Salter

Three views on British rearmament

The recruiting campaign for the Regular Army is not going well. What we want is a very definite statement from the Prime Minister that we need an Army. Then we can lay down what we want the Army for and how it is to be used.

From the private Diaries of the Late Field Marshal
The Lord Ironside G.C.B., C.M.G., D.S.O.
By permission of the Lord Ironside

We are now in the third year of openly avowed rearmament. Why is it, if all is going well, there are so many deficiencies? Why, for instance, are the Guards drilling with flags instead of machine guns and anti-tank rifles?

25th May 1938, Winston Churchill in the House of Commons

I wish we could rearm a little more quietly, but I suppose democracy is a bar to that. People in England are too much under the impression that Germany wants war.

9th March 1939, by Nevile Henderson
From BRITISH DOCUMENTS 3, VII

Chamberlain's views on running foreign policy given in the House of Commons, 3rd October 1938

Lasting peace is not to be obtained by sitting still and waiting for it to come. It requires active, positive efforts to secure it.

Lord Halifax's impressions of Germany, November 1937

Lord Halifax's general conclusion, therefore, was that the Germans had no policy of immediate adventure. They were too busy building up their country which was still in a state of revolution.

From a Cabinet memorandum

The Czech question—Nevile Henderson's view

I feel very strongly about the Sudeten question. Living as they do in solid block on the German frontier they have, in my opinion, a moral right to at least self-administration and eventually to self-determination. It is morally unjust to compel this solid Teutonic minority to remain subjected to a Slav government at Prague.

I do believe that once the Sudeten question is satisfactorily settled, Hitler would be quite willing to talk seriously.

7th April 1938, Letter from Berlin

The Munich Conference—Churchill's view given in the House of Commons, 5th October 1938

The German dictator, instead of snatching his victuals from the table, has been content to have them served to him course by course. I believe the Czechs, left to themselves, and told they were going to get no help from the Western Powers, would have been able to make better terms than they have got and they could hardly have worse.

The Munich Conference—view of 'The Times'

No conqueror returning from a victory on the battlefields has come home adorned with nobler laurels than Mr. Chamberlain from Munich yesterday.

1st October 1938, reprinted by permission

The German attack on Poland

For two whole days the wretched Poles had been bombed and massacred and we were still considering within what time limit Hitler should be invited to tell us whether he felt like relinquishing his prey. A year before the House had risen to its feet to give Chamberlain an ovation when he announced a last minute hope of peace. This time any similar announcement would have been met by a universal howl of execration.

Leo Amery (Conservative M.P.), MY POLITICAL LIFE VOL. III, 1939
Reprinted by permission of Hutchinson Publishing Group Ltd.

The declaration of war: Chamberlain broadcasts at 11.15 a.m. on 3rd September, 1939

You can imagine what a bitter blow it is for me that all my long struggle to win peace has failed. Yet I cannot believe there is anything more or anything different that I could have done and that would have been more successful. Up to the last it would have been quite possible to have arranged a peaceful and honourable settlement between Germany and Poland, but Hitler would not have it.

Books for Further Reading

Alford, B. W. E.	*Depression and Recovery?*	Macmillan 1972
Barnes and Middlemas	*Baldwin*	Weidenfeld and Nicolson 1969
Barnett, C.	*The Collapse of British Power*	Eyre Methuen 1972
Brand, C. F.	*Short History of the British Labour Party*	Stanford University Press 1965
Cowling, M.	*The Impact of Labour*	Cambridge University Press 1971
Cross, C.	*Philip Snowden*	Barrie and Jenkins 1966
Gilbert, B. B.	*Britain Since 1918*	Batsford 1967
Gilbert, B. B.	*British Social Policy 1914-1939*	Batsford 1970
Gilbert, M.	*Britain and Germany Between the Wars*	Longman 1964
Hobley, L. F.	*The Trade Union Story*	Blackie 1969
Hobley, L. F.	*Working Class and Democratic Movements*	Blackie 1970
James, R. R.	*Churchill. A Study in Failure 1900-1939*	Weidenfeld and Nicolson 1970
Marwick, A.	*Britain in the Century of Total War*	Bodley Head 1968
Montgomery, J.	*The Twenties*	Allen and Unwin 1957
Morgan, K. O.	*The Age of Lloyd George 1890-1929*	Allen and Unwin 1971
Mowat, C. L.	*Britain Between the Wars*	Methuen 1955
Pollard, S.	*The Development of the British Economy 1914-1935*	Arnold 1962
Raymond, J.	*The Baldwin Age*	Eyre and Spottiswoode 1960
Reynolds, P. A.	*British Foreign Policy in the Inter-War Years*	Longman 1954

Taylor, A. J. P.	*English History 1914-1945*	Oxford University Press 1965
Thompson, N.	*The Antiappeasers*	Oxford University Press 1971
Thorne, C.	*The Approach of War*	Macmillan 1967
Wilson, T.	*The Downfall of the Liberal Party 1914-1935*	Collins 1966

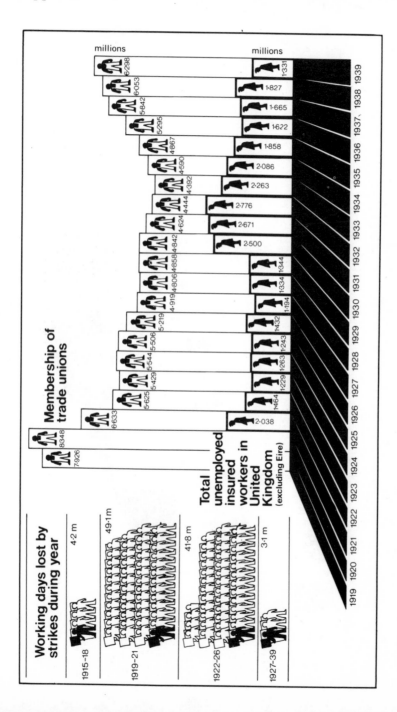

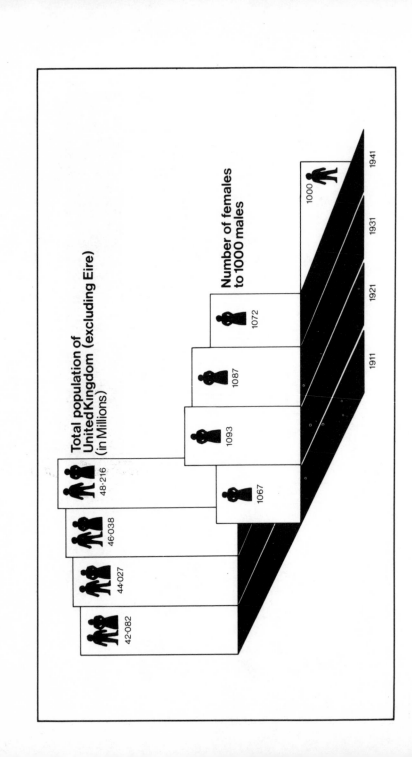

Total population of United Kingdom (excluding Eire) (in Millions)

42·082 44·027 46·038 48·216

Number of females to 1000 males

1067 1093 1087 1072 1000

1911 1921 1931 1941

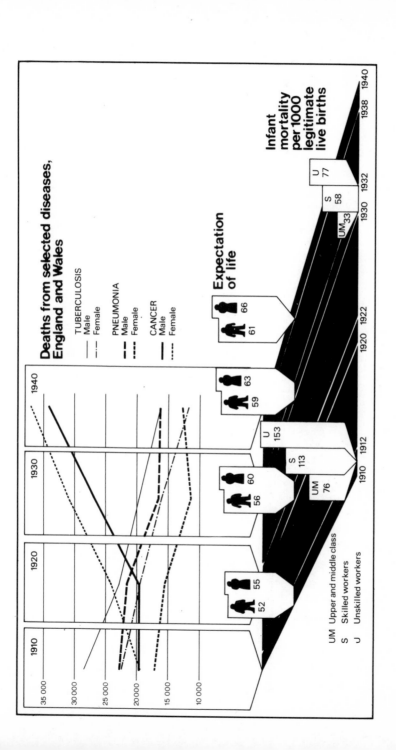

Deaths from selected diseases, England and Wales

TUBERCULOSIS
Male
Female

PNEUMONIA
Male
Female

CANCER
Male
Female

35 000
30 000
25 000
20 000
15 000
10 000

1910   1920   1930   1940

Expectation of life

Male 66
Female 61

Male 63
Female 59

Male 60
Female 56

Male 55
Female 52

1910   1912   1920   1922   1930   1932   1938   1940

Infant mortality per 1000 legitimate live births

U 153
S 113
UM 76

U 77
S 58
UM 33

UM Upper and middle class
S   Skilled workers
U   Unskilled workers

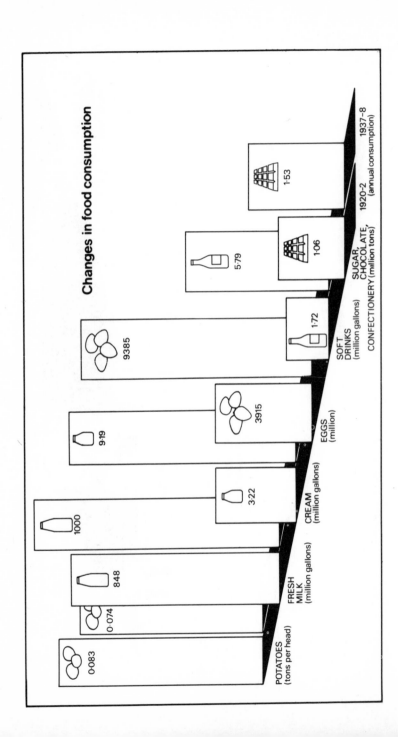

Changes in food consumption

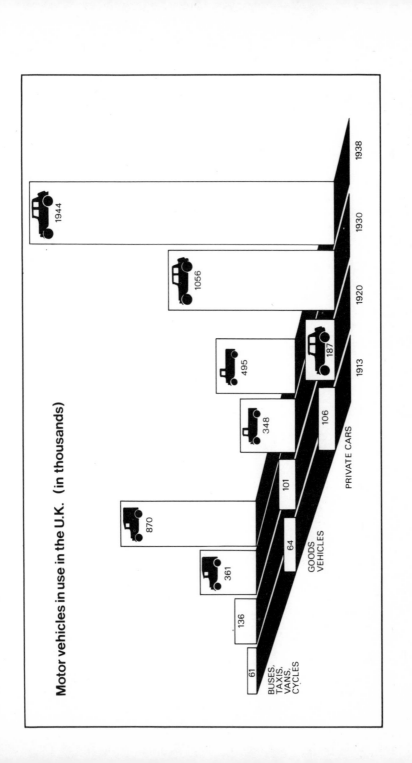

Motor vehicles in use in the U.K. (in thousands)

Index

TIME CHART———

1918
Feb. 6 Representation of the People Act
Nov. 11 Armistice ends Great War
Dec. 14 Coalition re-elected
1919
Jan.–Feb. Strikes in Glasgow and Belfast
June 28 Treaty of Versailles signed
Sep. 26–Oct. 5 Rail Strike
Nov. 28 Lady Astor first woman M.P.
1920
Jan. 10 League of Nations Covenant comes into being
Apr. 30 Conscription abolished
Aug. 9 General strike threat
Nov. Prices 176% above 1914
Dec. 23 Government of Ireland Act
1921
British Broadcasting Company formed
Mar. Mines returned to private owner-ship
Mar. 31 Miners locked out
Apr. 15 Black Friday
June 7 First Parliament of N. Ireland opens
July 11 British and Sinn Fein truce
Dec. 6 British–Irish peace treaty
1922
Feb. 24 Geddes 'axes' govt spending
Oct. 17 'Hunger March' begins in Glasgow
Oct. 24 Dail adopts constitution of Irish Free State
Nov. 14 BBC 2LO broadcasts
Nov. 17 Conservatives win General Election
Dec. 6–7 Irish Free State & N. Ireland in existence
Dec. 17 British troops leave Free State
Marie Stopes begins birth control campaign
1923
Apr. 28 First F.A. Cup Final
May 20 Bonar Law resigns due to ill health
May 22 Baldwin forms govt
July 2–Aug. 20 London bus strike
Dec. 6 Conservatives lose General Election
1924
Jan. 22 Baldwin resigns
Jan. 23 MacDonald forms first Lab. govt
Feb. 1 Britain recognizes U.S.S.R.
Feb. 16–26 Dock strike
Apr. 24 Irish boundary conference fails
Oct. 9 Parliament dissolved
Oct. 25 Zinoviev letter published
Oct. 29 Conservatives win General Election
Nov. 21 Baldwin repudiates treaty with U.S.S.R.
1925
Apr. 3 Gold Standard re-introduced
July 13 Govt enquiry into coal dispute

July 31 Mine owners subsized
Dec. 3 Irish boundaries finally settled
1926
Jan. 26 Baird demonstrates television
May 1 Miners locked out
May 3–12 General Strike
Oct. 9 Imperial Conference begins
Nov. 19 Miners accept wage cuts
1927
Jan. 1 British Broadcasting Corporation takes over
May 27 Britain breaks off diplomatic relations with U.S.S.R.
July 28 Trade Unions Act—general strikes illegal
The Jazz Singer first major sound film
1928
May 7 Votes for women at 21
Dec. 20 Britain recognizes Nanking govt of China
Fleming discovers penicillin
1929
June 5 MacDonald forms Lab. govt
Oct. 3 Britain resumes relations with U.S.S.R.
1930
Apr. 22 Britain, France, Italy, Japan & U.S.A. sign naval disarmament treaty
Oct. 1–Nov. 14 Imperial Conference in London
1931
Feb. Mosley forms New Party
July 25 May Committee forecasts £100 million deficit and proposes drastic cuts
Aug. 24 MacDonald resigns as Lab. P.M.
Aug. 25 MacDonald forms Nat. Govt
Sep. 10 Economy measures provoke riots in Glasgow and London
Sep. 15 Naval mutiny at Invergordon over pay cuts
Sep. 21 Britain abandons Gold Standard
Oct. 27 Nat. Govt wins 558 seats
The Means Test is introduced
Dec. 23 Statute of Westminster defines Dominion status
1932
Mar. 1 Protection in Britain—corn subsidies
Apr. 6 Minister of Health urges slum clearance
July 21 Imperial preference advocated
Sep. 28 Free trade liberals resign
Mosley forms British Union of Fascist
1933
Feb. 9 Oxford Union Society pass motion refusing to fight for King & Country
Feb. 16 Lab. Party censures govt for use of Poor Law against unemployed
July 15 Britain signs pact with France, Germany and Italy
Nov. 16 Lib. Party goes into opposition
Dec. 28 Last war-debt payment made to U.S.